UNIVERSITY OF NEW ENGLAND

MONOGRAPHS

II

J.D. Hainsworth

David Garrick: Selected Verse

THE PREPOSTEROUS HEAD DRESS
OR THE FEATHERED LADY
Published by Darly, 39, Strand, March 26, 1776

See Nos. 52 and 55

DAVID GARRICK

SELECTED VERSE

edited with an introduction and notes
by

J.D. HAINSWORTH

The University of New England
Armidale
Australia
1981

Distributed by the University of New England Publishing Unit

Printed by The University of New England.

Published by
The University of New England Publishing Unit,
The University of New England,
Armidale,
N.S.W. 2351,
Australia.

National Library of Australia
Cataloguing-in-Publication entry

Hainsworth, J.D., 1924 —
David Garrick: Selected Verse.

(University of New England monographs : 2)
Bibliography
ISBN 0 85834 347 9
ISBN 0 85834 348 7 Paperback
ISSN 0 75—5994

1. Garrick, David, 1717-1779—Selected Verse.
I. Title (Series)

016.780924

ACKNOWLEDGEMENTS

My first acknowledgement must be to Mary E. Knapp, to whose *Checklist of Verse by David Garrick* (Charlottesville, 1955) and *Prologues and Epilogues of the Eighteenth-Century* (New Haven, 1961) I am much indebted. While I was working on this selection, Miss Knapp was revising the *Checklist* and she generously made available to me her latest findings.

Other major debts, as far as modern printed works are concerned, are to *The Letters of David Garrick*, ed. David M. Little and George M. Kahrl (Cambridge, Mass., 1963) and to those volumes of *The London Stage* (Carbondale, 1960-68) concerned with the period during which Garrick was writing, which are edited by George Winchester Stone, Jr.

I wish to express my thanks to Professor J.P. Hardy for his steady encouragement and for practical advice on editorial procedures. I am indebted also, for assistance with research, to Mrs. Catharine Clarke and Mr. James Baxendale. I wish to thank the Publications Committee of the University of New England, whose support has made possible the publication of this work, and also the University's Publishing Unit, for friendly co-operation. I owe a particular debt of gratitude to my wife, who has patiently sustained my immersion in the subject-matter of this book, and who has stood in as researcher, copyist, collator of texts or typist, whenever a need has arisen.

I am grateful for permission to copy from manuscripts in the possession of the Henry W. and Albert A. Berg Collections at the New York Public Library, and of the Folger Shakespeare Library, Washington, D.C. For access to manuscripts and early printed items I am indebted also to: the Australian National Library, Canberra; the Bath Municipal Libraries; the de Beer Collection, University of Otago Library, Dunedin, New Zealand; the Beinecke Rare Book and Manuscript Library, Yale University; the Birmingham Public Libraries; the Bodleian Library, Oxford; the British Library; Cambridge University Library; Columbia University Library, New York City; the Dixson Library, University of New England, Armidale, N.S.W.; Edinburgh University Library; the Fisher Library, University of Sydney; the Forster Collection, Victoria and Albert Museum, London; the Library of the Honourable Society of Gray's Inn, London; the Guildhall Library, London; the Harvard Theatre Collection, Harvard College Library; the Houghton Library, Harvard University; the Henry E. Huntington Library and Art Gallery, San Marino, California; the Library of the University of London; the Osborn Collection, Yale University Library; the State Library of New South Wales, Sydney; the New York Historical Society; the Regenstein Library, University of Chicago; the National Library of Scotland; the Library of the University of Sheffield; the Library of Congress, Washington, D.C.; the State Library of Victoria, Melbourne.

The Introduction to this volume is based on a paper which I gave at the Second David Nichol Smith Seminar at Canberra in 1970, and which appears in *Studies in the Eighteenth Century, II*, ed. R.F. Brissenden, Canberra, 1973.

J.D. Hainsworth,
University of New England,
Armidale, N.S.W.

CONTENTS

INTRODUCTION

David Garrick will be known as an actor for as long as the English theatre continues to exist. As a theatre manager he is remembered for the innovations, notably in stage lighting and scenic design, that were introduced at Drury Lane during his management. As a playwright he survives still — if only because of *The Clandestine Marriage* written in collaboration with George Colman the elder. His brilliance as a letter-writer is evident in the three-volume edition of his letters brought out by D.M. Little and G.M. Kahrl in 1963.[1] And, of course, he is known as an associate of Dr Johnson and a member of the famous Club. But David Garrick as a poet? This aspect of his achievement has been almost lost sight of. Yet verse-writing was an activity that he persisted in throughout his busy and successful life. "It seems," says his friend and biographer Arthur Murphy, "that his close connection with Dr. Johnson at Litchfield [*sic*], gave him an early turn for versification . . . . If we except the pleasures he enjoyed in conversation with his friends, poetical composition was his chief recreation from the fatigue of his profession."[2] There has been no new edition of these poems since Kearsley published *The Poetical Works of David Garrick, Esq.* in 1785. Mary E. Knapp, it is true, brought out a check-list in 1955,[3] and lists, in all, 479 items,[4] many of them unknown to Kearsley. But the only other significant recognition of Garrick as a poet that I know of has come from David Nichol Smith, who includes two items by him in *The Oxford Book of Eighteenth Century Verse.*[5] One of his choices is the song Garrick wrote for his patriotic pantomime *Harlequin's Invasion*, usually known by the first line of its chorus, "Heart of Oak", and so traditional that its authorship has been widely forgotten. Nichol Smith's other choice is two stanzas of Garrick's poem "To Mr. Gray, on the Publication of His Odes":

> Repine not, Gray, that our weak dazzled eyes
> Thy daring heights and brightness shun;
> How few can track the eagle to the skies,
> Or like him gaze upon the sun!
>
> The gentle reader loves the gentle Muse,
> That little dares, and little means,
> Who humbly sips her learning from *Reviews*,
> Or flutters in the *Magazines*.

---

[1] *The Letters of David Garrick*, Cambridge, Mass., 1963.

[2] Arthur Murphy, *The Life of David Garrick*, London, 1801, II, 187-88.

[3] Mary E. Knapp, *A Checklist of Verse by David Garrick*, Charlottesville, 1955.

[4] A few items are listed more than once, under different titles. On the other hand, this number does not include all the songs Garrick wrote for musical plays.

[5] Nos. 263 and 264.

These lines constitute a polished and dignified compliment. For the modern reader, however, what is actually said about Gray and his odes is, perhaps, too vague and general. This is a failing typical of Garrick as a writer of verse, whenever he ventures outside the field of light verse. From his *Ode on the Death of Mr. Pelham*, for instance, no impression emerges of an individual person or even a recognizable type. The deceased prime minister is merely idealized:

> No selfish views to oppress mankind,
> No mad ambition fired thy mind,
>   To purchase fame with blood;
> Thy bosom glowed with purer heat,
> Convinced that to be truly great
>   Is only to be good.

And in the "Ode" on Shakespeare that Garrick wrote to be delivered by himself at the Shakespeare Jubilee at Stratford-on-Avon in 1769, where he would surely have wished to be at his best, there is nothing beyond uninspired commonplace.

Garrick was more in his element with satirical verse. His mock epitaph on Goldsmith was delivered extempore at a meeting of the Club:

> Here lies Nolly Goldsmith, for shortness called Noll,
> Who wrote like an angel but talked like poor Poll.[6]

Another extempore composition was Garrick's couplet on Dr. John Hill, the well-known purveyor of medicines, who had reviled the Drury Lane management after his farce *The Rout* had been badly received:

> For physic and farces his equal there scarce is;
> His farces are physic, his physic a farce is.

Such verse as this is an extension of conversational wit, and so strongly suggestive of its social origin that one is tempted to speculate on who was present in the company that first heard it.

This connection with society is not, of course, something peculiar to the verse of Garrick. A great deal of — and, indeed, the best of — the poetry of the eighteenth century was written as a celebration of social life. Verse forms almost unknown today — epigrams, mock epitaphs, verse letters, prologues,

---

[6]In his edition of *The Works of Oliver Goldsmith* (London, 1854, I, 78), Peter Cunningham prints, from "the original in Garrick's own handwriting", both the epigram and Garrick's account of how it came to be composed.

epilogues, etc. — were popular because they were appropriate to this kind of celebration. In some of these forms Garrick excelled. If the excellence in question is of a kind that literary critics of our own day do not set great store by, it is nevertheless true that Garrick's verse continued to find enthusiastic readers for several decades after his death. For the modern reader it can, at the very least, provide an introduction to the society of his time which is just as illuminating as that provided by its journals and memoirs, its architecture and its landscape gardens.

Garrick has another piece relating to the affair of John Hill and his farce. This shows his muse *fluttering* "in the Magazines". It makes use of the fact that, at the first performance of *The Rout*, the playwright's name had been withheld, and he had been designated merely as "A Person of Honour":

> Says a friend to the Doctor, "Pray give it about
> That this farce is not yours, or the house will not fill;
> What had come of your *nerves*, or your *pox*, or your *gout*,
> Had these embryos crawled forth as begot by John Hill?
> Let your Muse, as your pamphlets, come forth, I advise ye,
> Like a goddess of old with a cloud cast upon her."
> "You're right," quoth the Doctor, "and more to disguise me,
> I'll give myself out for a Person of Honour."

It may be objected that this is still witticism rather than wit, in any literary sense of the term. It is, indeed, instructive to set these lines beside Charles Churchill's account of Hill in *The Rosciad*. Churchill's superiority is that his lines are more than just witticism: they make a statement more complex than Garrick's and they use the peculiar resources of poetry to achieve their complexity. Churchill's account of Hill is accurate enough: he had been an actor, if not a very successful one; he had contributed a regular letter entitled "The Inspector" to *The London Daily Advertiser*; and he was a botanist of distinction, as well as a medical man. A cursory glance might even give the impression that Churchill was praising Hill, as he reminds us of these remarkably varied achievements.

> For who, like him, his various pow'rs could call
> Into so many shapes, and shine in all?
> Who could so nobly grace the motley list,
> Actor, Inspector, Doctor, Botanist?[7]

The use of the word "shapes", however, makes one think of an actor or a mimic changing his shape, and suggests that there is an element of pretence in Hill's achievements.[8] And "motley", of course, as well as meaning "diverse",

---

[7]*The Poetical Works of Charles Churchill*, ed. Douglas Grant, Oxford, 1956,p. 6, lines 109-12.

[8]For this sense of "shapes" cf. *The Rosciad*, 395-96, on Samuel Foote as actor and mimic:
> By turns transform'd into all kinds of shapes, ·
> Constant to none, F[OO]TE laughs, cries, struts, and scrapes.

carries a suggestion of folly. The falling rhythm (trochees and dactyls) of the fourth line clashes sharply with the rising iambic rhythm that has conveyed a sense of achievement in the three preceding lines. The impression one is finally left with is that Hill deserves a certain amount of credit for all that he has done, but not so much as he himself would claim. One is made to feel, too, that the poet is carefully weighing what he says, and so deserves to be taken seriously. The poetry here is by no means as complex as that of Dryden's portrait of Zimri in *Absolam and Achitophel*, which the passage recalls, but it *is* poetry. The use of language is richer and more subtle than in Garrick's epigram.

It is not, of course, fair to show up the deficiencies of Garrick's verse by comparing lines he wrote for a newspaper with an extract from a consciously literary work like *The Rosciad*. A fairer comparison would be between *The Rosciad* and Garrick's poem *The Fribbleriad*, which is a contribution to that mock-heroic genre to which *The Rosciad* also belongs. Garrick's poem was a rejoinder to attacks made on his abilities as an actor by a certain Thomas Fitzpatrick, under various pseudonyms such as "XYZ". Fitzpatrick and his associates are portrayed as effeminate "fribbles", whose quarrel with Garrick is that he has made fun of their kind while performing the role of Fribble in his play *Miss in Her Teens*. Early in Garrick's poem, Fitzpatrick's motives are questioned:

> Say, Garrick, does he write for bread,
> This friend of yours, this XYZ?
> For pleasure sure, not bread — 'twere vain
> To write for that he ne'er could gain:
> No calls of nature to excuse him,
> He deals in rancour to amuse him.

Fizgig, Fitzpatrick's representative in the poem, is portrayed as:

> one larger than the rest,
> With visage sleek and swelling chest,
> With stretched-out fingers and a thumb
> Stuck to his hips, and jutting bum.

Called to take the chair at a meeting of fribbles,

> He smiled and to the honoured seat
> Paddled away with mincing feet.
> So have I seen on dove-house top,
> With cocked-up tail and swelling crop,
> A pouting pigeon waddling run,
> Shuffling, wriggling, noddling on.

As these extracts illustrate, Garrick's rhymes are clever enough, his mock-heroic devices are effective, and his tetrameters create the impression intended of

The total effect, however, is simply to deflate, to ridicule, to denigrate. The more serious and complex kind of statement that Churchill has achieved is not attempted.

One has to go to Garrick's prologues and epilogues to find a complexity in any way approaching Churchill's. It is on these theatrical pieces that Garrick's claim to be remembered for his verse must mainly rest. And yet, of course, the complexity there achieved is not of the same kind as that to be found in a literary work like *The Rosciad*. For the prologues and epilogues are not literature but drama. They were part of that varied theatrical entertainment that, in Garrick's day, stretched from six at night until about eleven, and included — in addition to the comedy or tragedy that was the mainpiece for the evening — music, singing or dancing, and an afterpiece, usually a short farce. Being theatrical entertainment, prologues and epilogues are not meant just to be read with the eye, nor even just to be recited to a company; they are meant to be performed to an audience. The medium is not just words, but words acted: it is not just the voice of an actor that is required, but his whole person and personality. For example, in Mrs. Frances Sheridan's comedy *The Discovery*, Sir Anthony Branville is an elderly beau who, in spite of his age, manages to fall in love with two women. The method Garrick had hit on of playing this character involved a deliberate checking of the movement of his face and body, to achieve a startling contrast between Sir Anthony's passionate sentiments and the calm voice and stiffly formal mien in which he uttered them, and an equally sharp contrast with the extreme mobility of face and body that usually characterised Garrick's acting. "Sir Anthony Branville's Address to the Ladies" — an epilogue which Garrick wrote for Mrs. Sheridan's play — gives him a further opportunity to exploit this way of acting. Such a piece is designed to create an audience, which is not just a company of people assembled in an auditorium, but a company of people controlled and transformed by the arts of dramatist and actor. Stepping right out of the play, Sir Anthony now subjects the ladies of the audience to his decorous blandishments:

> Ladies, before I go, will you allow
> A most devoted slave to make his bow?
> Brought to your bar, ye most angelic jury
> 'Tis you shall try me for my amorous fury.
> Have I been guilty, pray, of indecorum?
> My ardours were so fierce I could not lower 'em.
> Such raging passions I confess an evil;
> In flesh and blood like mine they play the devil.
> Bound on the rack of love poor I was laid,
> Between two fires, a widow and a maid.
> My heart, poor scorched dove, now pants for rest;
> Where, ladies, shall the flutterer find a nest?
> Take pity, fair ones, on the tortured thing,

Heal it and let it once more chirp and sing.
Yet to approach you were infatuation.
If souls like mine, so prone to inflammation,
Should meet your tinder hearts there would be conflagration.
Indeed, so prudent are most men of fashion,
They run no danger for they feel no passion.
Though fairest faces smile, they can defy 'em,
Though softest tongues should plead, they can deny 'em;
Mankind would cease but for such loving fools as I am.

Twice in the last eight lines quoted, a triplet occurs in which feminine rhyme-words lead on to an alexandrine and a pause which effectively takes in, and, indeed, stimulates laughter. So wholly dramatic is this piece that an audience is implied even in the movement of the verse.

Dramatic as Garrick's prologues and epilogues are, they are not dramatic in quite the same way that a play is dramatic. For a play involves a sustained fiction: the actor maintains his role; the audience is continually encouraged to give credence to a fictitious world. There is always an element of fiction in a prologue or epilogue, even when the speaker addresses the audience in his own person. For he is pretending to speak his thoughts extempore, whereas, in fact, they have been carefully prepared and versified; and they are not his own thoughts, either, unless author and speaker happen to be the same person. Yet the fiction is never so dominant as in a play, for even when the speaker of an epilogue acts the role he has just been playing, as in "Sir Anthony Branville's Address to the Ladies", he is now in a different and more personal relationship with the audience, addressing them directly from the apron, and sometimes with the curtain dropped behind him.

"Sir Anthony Branville's Address" illustrates particularly well this incompleteness of the fiction. It was not attached to Mrs. Sheridan's comedy until this was revived in 1776, thirteen years after the first production. The original epilogue had been spoken by Mrs. Pritchard, who was now dead. Indeed, Garrick, as Sir Anthony, was the only one of the original performers left. For some of the audience, at any rate, Garrick would stand before them, not just as Sir Anthony, but also as the sole survivor and representative of the original cast.

The epilogue to the tragedy of *Barbarossa* shows Garrick again exploiting the ambiguity of the speaker's role. Here, Henry Woodward, in the character of a fine gentleman, expresses his doubts whether the kind of fare they have just been having — tragedy — is really suited to an English audience. The effectiveness of his conclusion comes from the audience's awareness that the actor, who is an author as well, has a vested interest in the recommendations made by the character he is playing:

Banish your gloomy scenes to foreign climes,
Reserve alone to bless these golden times
A farce or two — and Woodward's pantomimes.

Another variation on this effect is in the prologue Garrick wrote for Arthur Murphy's *The Desert Island*. Here Garrick appears as "a drunken poet" — the author of a play, which, he says, the manager has not the wit to put on, though it compares very favourably with the play that is about to be performed. After a little flattery of the audience in an attempt to raise funds so that his play may be published by subscription, the drunken author staggers off stage exclaiming to himself "A little flattery sometimes does well", a line from Colley Cibber's version of Shakespeare's *Richard III*,[9] the play in which Garrick first established his reputation as an actor, in a role vastly different from the one he is playing now. The audience's applause would be the louder for this reminder of Garrick's past achievements and his extraordinary versatility.

In the writing of prologues and epilogues, certain problems were involved that were common to all those who attempted them at that time. Not the least of these arose simply from the fact that the custom of having prologues and epilogues had lasted for so long. Already, by 1704 even, Nicholas Rowe, in the epilogue to his play *The Biter*, was complaining about this:

> OF all the Taxes which the Poet pays,
> Those Funds of Verse, none are so hard to raise
> As Prologues and as Epilogues to Plays.
> So many mighty Wits are gone before,
> Th' have rifled all the Muses sacred Store.[10]

By the time of Garrick the variations in approach that were within the scope of a prologue or epilogue writer had been virtually exhausted. In these circumstances the writer deserves credit for the extent to which he is able to give new life to a stock device. Thus, the incongruity of the convention that the tragic heroine should rise from death to deliver a comic epilogue had been turned into a source of laughter by John Dryden in 1669, in his notorious epilogue to *Tyrannic Love*[11]. There, after Nell Gwynn, as tragic heroine, had been slain, she resisted attempts to carry her off stage, exclaiming to one of the bearers:

> Hold, are you mad? you damn'd confounded Dog,
> I am to rise, and speak the Epilogue.

As late as 1756, in the epilogue to *Athelstan* spoken by Mrs. Cibber, Garrick is still able successfully to make fun out of the incongruity — paradoxically

---

[9] Noted   by Mary E. Knapp, *Prologues and Epilogues of the Eighteenth Century*, New Haven, 1961, p. 103.

[10] Quoted Knapp, *Prologues and Epilogues*, p. 24.

[11] *The Poems and Fables of John Dryden*, ed. James Kinsley, London, 1961, p. 119.

by introducing into the situation another old joke — one about women's talkativeness. Each joke provides the other with a new context. The listener is agreeably surprised, and amused, that they can still be freshened up in this way.

> To speak ten words, again I've fetched my breath,

says Mrs. Cibber, the deceased tragic heroine:

> The tongue of woman struggles hard with death.

Another hackneyed device is where it is pretended that the prologue meant for the evening has been lost, and therefore the actual prologue really is an extempore effusion, and is not just pretending to be one. Garrick puts this device to brilliant use in his prologue to the tragedy of *Barbarossa*. Before the play, a serving-lad enters in search of his master, the author of the play, who is wanted urgently because he has the script of the prologue in his pocket. The lad, who is from the country, expresses his astonishment at what he sees from the stage:

> Law, what a crowd is here! What noise and pother!
> Fine lads and lasses one o' top o' t'other.
> *(Pointing to the rows of pit and gallery)*
> I could for ever here with wonder geaze.
> I ne'er saw church so full in all my days.

This leads him on to tell of other astonishing experiences that have befallen him since he came to London: how he has fled from the service of his first employer on seeing him eat turtle:

> Law, how I stared! I thought — who knows but I,
> For want of monsters may be made a pie.

His second master, a lord, has offended him by his total absorption in card-playing. His third was a lady:

> A lady next, who liked a smart young lad,
> Hired me forthwith, but, troth, I thought her mad.
> She turned the world top down, as I may say;
> She changed the day to neet, the neet to day.
> I stood one day with coach and did but stoop
> To put the foot-board down, and with her hoop
> She covered me all o'er. Where are you, lout?
> Here ma'am, says I, for heaven's sake let me out.
> I was so sheamed with all her freakish ways,
> She wore her gear so short, so low her stays —
> Fine folks show all for nothing nowadays.

Now he is "the poet's man". His wages depend on this night's venture. If it is not successful, he will "pack up all, and whistle whoame again." The young lad from the country was played by Garrick, who showed off his versatility as an actor in the tragedy that followed – where, as Selim, a king's son of Algiers, he overthrew the tyrant who had murdered his father and planned to ravish his mother. In the epilogue of this play, the fine gentleman played by Woodward, who forces his way on to the stage to protest against the country boy's criticisms of upper-class life, provides yet another variation on the pretence that this is not the speech intended.

Another device popular with prologue-writers was to make the speaker, who could see the audience, since the candles in the house were lit throughout the evening, address the various sections of it separately. Garrick does this in the epilogue that he wrote for Mrs. Cibber to the tragedy of *Virginia*, and, in doing so, he brings out vividly the audience's diversity. In the shilling seats in the upper gallery are the poorer folk:

> No high-bred prudery in your region lurks,
> You boldly laugh and cry as nature works.

From among the middle-class spectators of the middle gallery, "some maiden dames" are picked out:

> So very chaste, they live in constant fears,
> And apprehension strengthens with their years.

In the boxes are the "Fine ladies", and in the pit the men of fashion:

> Ye bucks, who from the pit your terrors send.

Also in the pit, as other epilogues inform us, was the more critical and intellectual part of the audience.

In the writing of prologues and epilogues, the various and sometimes conflicting predilections and prejudices of the audience had to be taken note of, and, as far as possible, reconciled. For instance, the moral scruples of the middle-class "citizens", for a long time now an important element in the audience, had to be propitiated. So, in speaking Garrick's epilogue to Hoadly's *The Suspicious Husband*, Mrs. Pritchard abandons the role of the gay young Clarinda she has just been playing:

> Though the young smarts, I see, begin to sneer,
> And the old sinners cast a wicked leer,
> Be not alarmed, ye fair – you've nought to fear.
> No wanton hint, no loose ambiguous sense
> Shall flatter vicious taste at your expense.

Political and religious sensitivities, too, had to be carefully considered, for on these issues Garrick's audience was easily roused to violence. James

Boswell and two of his friends brought cudgels, not to mention catcalls, with them, when they went to the opening of *Elvira*, a tragedy by David Mallet, a free thinker and supporter of the unpopular minister, the Earl of Bute.[12] Garrick put on a *Chinese Festival* at Drury Lane in November, 1755, when feeling against the French was running high. Chinese the Festival may have been, but the company of dancers involved in it came from Paris. Fighting broke out between pro-French aristocrats and enraged patriots, severe damage was done to the theatre, and even the windows of Garrick's house were smashed. No doubt it was partly as a discouragement to such excesses that patriotic sentiments had become so conventional an ingredient in prologues and epilogues. Garrick's prologue to Mallet's masque, *Britannia*, in the writing of which Mallet also seems to have had a hand, is jingoistic in a more than usually clever way. Garrick staggers on stage as a drunken British sailor who says he has promised to take his girlfriend to a show before going back to beat the French. He chooses the tragedy of *Zara*, the mainpiece at Drury Lane that evening, because of the similarity of its name to that of his girl-friend, Sarah. The masque that is to accompany the tragedy also arouses his enthusiasm:

> But what is here so very large and plain?
> Bri-tan-nia — oh Britannia! — good again.
> Huzza, boys! By the Royal George I swear,
> Tom coxon and the crew shall straight be there.
> All free-born souls must take Bri-tan-nia's part,
> And give her three round cheers, with hand and heart.

No doubt, as Miss Knapp has suggested,[13] this display of patriotism was occasioned by a regrettable fact: that the tragedy of *Zara* was translated from the French!

Prologues and epilogues had to be appropriate to their speakers as well as to the audience. The choice of speakers was limited to some extent by convention. They were drawn from the leading members of the company. A prologue was almost invariably assigned to an actor, and an epilogue to an actress, though it could be given to a comic actor instead. The prologue or epilogue was generally considered to belong to the actor or actress it was first assigned to. If it was called for again after the first three nights of a play's run, the regular occasions when prologue and epilogue were attached to a play, then that particular actor or actress had to deliver it. A story is told of Tom King's being summoned from home late at night to repeat, at the insistence of the audience, who sat waiting for him, a prologue he had given

---

[12] See *Boswell's London Journal, 1762-1763*, ed. Frederick A. Pottle, London, 1950, pp. 152, 154-55.

[13] *Prologues and Epilogues*, p. 38.

earlier in the evening. Says King, in the prologue Garrick wrote for Colman's farce *The Spleen:*

> While living call me, for your pleasure use me;
> Should I tip off, I hope you'll then excuse me.

This is Garrick dramatising Tom King's own humorous and likeable character. He often does this for a speaker when he has no fictitious role for him. Another example is the epilogue he wrote for Mrs. Woffington to speak at the opening of Garrick's first season in management, in 1747. Here Mrs. Woffington, whose fondness for the opposite sex was notorious, is made to complain against the new policy of prohibiting public access behind the scenes:

> Each actress now a locked-up nun must be,
> And priestly managers must keep the key.

It was Mrs. Woffington who, flushed with her success in the part of Sir Harry Wildair, boasted to James Quin that half the town believed her to be a man. "Madam," replied Quin, "the other half know you to be a woman."[14] In the epilogue in question, Garrick was actually trying to gain acceptance for the policy he makes Mrs. Woffington complain of. He hoped, unrealistically as it turned out, that opposition would be dissolved by laughter.

In the skill with which he tailors prologues and epilogues to their speakers, Garrick is without rival. This is hardly surprising, since his success as a manager depended on his being able to gauge with accuracy the abilities of actors and actresses. An interesting illustration of the pains Garrick would take in this matter is the epilogue he wrote for Mrs. Pritchard on her retirement from the stage. To try to ensure her satisfaction, in the copy of the epilogue he sent her, he marked lines she could omit if she wished, and offered variant readings.[15] Knowing that Mrs. Pritchard will be deeply moved by the occasion, he makes her say:

> I now appear myself, distressed, dismayed,
> More than in all the characters I've played.

And the epilogue is so worded that any tears she sheds will help rather than hinder the effect aimed at. "She spoke her farewell epilogue," says Thomas Davies, "with many sobs and tears, which were increased by the generous feelings of a numerous and splendid audience."[16]

---

[14] Murphy, *Life*, I, 37.

[15] See *Letters of David Garrick*, No. 498.

[16] *Memoirs of the Life of David Garrick, Esq.*, 3rd ed., London, 1781, II, 189.

It was obviously important that a piece should make no demands that were beyond the speaker's competence — that an epilogue for Mrs. Cibber, for instance, whose gifts lay in tragedy, should not demand too much in the way of comic acting. It was no less desirable that speakers should be given a chance to display their own special abilities. Of particular interest, from this point of view, are the prologues and epilogues which Garrick wrote to deliver himself. It was in his ability to transform himself physically, rather than in the vocal aspects of acting, that Garrick's greatest excellence lay. "Damn him," exclaimed Mrs. Clive, "I believe he could act a gridiron."[17] The point of this remark is that a gridiron does not talk — Garrick did not need speech to create a role. The Rev. William Mason remarks particularly on Garrick's powers of facial expression, and says he "disliked to perform any part whatever, where expression of countenance was not more necessary than recitation of sentiment."[18] The epilogue by Garrick for his own farce The Lying Valet provides supporting evidence in this matter. It is an apology for his behaviour in the play by its leading character, the Lying Valet, played by the author. In illustrating how widespread is the vice of lying, Garrick passes rapidly through impersonations of a gouty lawyer, a dishonest doctor, a boastful author, and Lady Dainty, a pretended prude, switching to and fro between these and his basic role of valet. Finally he gives himself the opportunity to hit off a Dutchman, a Frenchman, a German and a Spaniard, all within the space of two lines. One is reminded of Johnson's reply to a remark by Dr. Burney that Garrick's face was beginning to look old: "Why, Sir, you are not to wonder at that; no man's face has had more wear and tear."[19] Garrick's prologue to Much Ado About Nothing, written twenty-four years later, for a Royal Command performance that marked his return to the stage after eighteen months abroad, is only slightly less exacting. It allows him to impersonate a truant schoolboy returning fearfully to school, a "youth of parts" cocking his glass at the aging Garrick in the street and commenting on his fatness, and, finally, a Chelsea pensioner, still ready, like Garrick himself, to serve his King:

> Should the drum beat to arms, at first he'll grieve
> For wooden leg, lost eye and armless sleeve;
> Then cocks his hat, looks fierce and swells his chest:
> " 'Tis for my King, and, zounds, I'll do my best!"

The prologue to the Royal Command performance of Much Ado About Nothing was written to be performed by a particular actor and tailored to his particular abilities; it was also written for one particular, and in this case,

---

[17]Quoted Percy Fitzgerald, The Life of Mrs. Catherine Clive, London, 1888, p. 77.

[18]Quoted James Boaden, Memoirs of Mrs. Siddons, London, 1827, II, 162-63.

[19]Boswell, Life of Johnson, ed. G.B. Hill, rev. L.F. Powell, Oxford, 1934-50, II, 410.

non-recurrent occasion, and for one quite specific audience.[20] These limitations, though present here in an extreme form, in some measure affected all prologue writers. The preoccupation with what was particular was a restriction the writer must necessarily accept, but for Garrick it was also a source of strength. For one thing, it helped to prevent the vagueness that is so often a fault in his non-dramatic verse; for another, no one understood better than he did the tendencies of the audience, the potentialities of the speakers, the subtle and ambiguous relationship that existed between one and the other, and all the particular circumstances of the theatre where he was manager, principal actor and occasional dramatist, as well as purveyor-in-chief of prologues and epilogues.

His intimate and many-sided knowledge of his theatre provided Garrick with a much firmer foundation for his poetry than any literary tradition could do — which is, no doubt, the main reason why these theatrical pieces are, generally, superior to anything else he wrote. This is the basis, too, for his eminence, if not pre-eminence, amongst writers in this genre. Dr. Johnson even compared him favourably with Dryden: "Dryden has written prologues superior to any that David Garrick has written; but David Garrick has written more good prologues than Dryden has done."[21] With the first part of this statement there can be no quarrelling. For sheer dramatic effectiveness, nothing in Garrick can quite equal, for instance, Dryden's epilogue to *An Evening's Love*.[22] Here the way the actress mimics the audience's behaviour and makes fun of its critical attitudes allows her to show off her abilities, and, at the same time, involves the audience, in a delightfully provocative way, in her performance. She also makes them laugh at French manners, but wittily justifies the author's borrowing of a French plot. If she is a good deal more bawdy than Garrick could permit, the bawdiness is made to seem not adventitious, but a genuine and amusing revelation of the speaker's character. Dryden shows in this epilogue that he can excel Garrick even in those dramatic qualities where Garrick is strongest. The first part of Dr. Johnson's verdict is unassailable, therefore. It is doubtful, however, if the second part of it — that "David Garrick has written more good prologues than Dryden has done" — is soundly based in arithmetical calculations. But whatever Garrick's status relative to Dryden, or, indeed, to anyone else, there are reasons enough why a modern reader might find a study of his prologues and epilogues worthwhile. Many of them still make lively and enjoyable reading — that is one reason. But for anyone interested in the history of the theatre they have

---

[20] It was, however, repeated when Garrick next played Benedick, on November 22nd 1765, and it was called for by the audience when he played Sir John Brute in Vanbrugh's *The Provoked Wife* on December 5th. See textual note on 37.

[21] Boswell, *Life*, II, 325.

[22] *The Poems and Fables of John Dryden*, 123-24.

a special importance. In them, in quite a unique way, the dead facts of history are brought to life again. As Garrick himself has pointed out in his prologue to *The Clandestine Marriage*, the art of the actor lacks the durability of other arts:

> The painter dead, yet still he charms the eye;
> While England lives his fame can never die.
> But he, who struts his hour upon the stage
> Can scarce extend his fame for half an age;
> Nor pen nor pencil can the actor save,
> The art and artist share one common grave.

Prologues and epilogues — and especially those of Garrick — to some extent ameliorate this situation. In them, so carefully tailored, as they often are, to the aptitudes of a particular speaker, there is captured something, at least, of the art and stage personality of the dead performer. Also accessible through them is the audience to which they were originally addressed — and to which they were also tailored. And this is not just because of the vivid portraits of that audience which they occasionally provide, but in a more existential way, too. For the imaginative reading and re-reading of these verses provide the nearest possible approximation to actually becoming oneself a part of that eighteenth-century audience. They bring to life for the reader a theatrical community, and this not in any merely external way, but by enabling him to feel for himself the tensions within it, by giving him a personal and unique experience of its intimate life.

A NOTE ON THE TEXTS

Poems by David Garrick are extant both in manuscript and in printed versions. Some of those in manuscript are merely copies of printed versions made by collectors or admirers. Others, however, were originally in the possession of Garrick himself, and are either autographs, or transcripts made at his direction, often with autograph revisions. The manuscripts in the Larpent Collection of the Huntington Library are in a special category. These are manuscripts which were submitted to the Lord Chamberlain, whose responsibility it was to censor prologues and epilogues, as well as the plays with which they were associated. The manuscripts of prologues and epilogues by Garrick in this collection do not, however, necessarily incorporate his final revisions. He would sometimes go on revising a prologue or epilogue after a copy of the play had been sent to the censor, and, indeed, sometimes even after the prologue or epilogue had already been delivered on one or more occasions. Thus, on November 9th 1774, he writes to Mrs. Abington suggesting an alteration to the epilogue to *The Maid of the Oaks*, which she would already have performed twice (see *Letters*, No. 869).

The printed texts of Garrick's verse vary in their authoritativeness.

There is no reason to doubt that, with such poems as the *Ode on the Death of Mr. Pelham* and *The Fribbleriad*, Garrick exercised supervision over the text that was printed. Indeed, the edition of *The Fribbleriad* includes a list of errors which, it is said, was drawn up by the author. With prologues and epilogues, it is reasonable to assume that, generally, a text printed with the first edition of a play represents Garrick's final version. If the procedure adopted with Burgoyne's *The Maid of the Oaks* was typical, then the copy for the first edition was sent to the printer directly from the theatre, after the playwright had been allowed an opportunity of looking it over (see *The Private Correspondence of David Garrick*, ed. James Boaden, London 1831-32, II, 18). It appears that sometimes, however, a prologue or epilogue was altered after the copy had been sent to the printer for the first edition, and, in such cases, a later edition of the play may give a later version. The versions of prologues and epilogues printed in newspapers and periodicals are frequently inaccurate. One is sometimes driven to the conclusion that a prologue or epilogue has been taken down in the theatre in inadequate shorthand by someone who did not hear accurately everything that was said. Journals, of course, copied from each other as well. In assembling his *Poetical Works of David Garrick* six years after the author's death, George Kearsley directed his efforts at achieving as complete a collection of Garrick's verse as possible, rather than at establishing the most authoritative texts of the poems printed:

> Abandoned and neglected as these [Garrick's poems] have been, both by their author and his representatives, the publisher has been prevailed upon to solicit the assistance of many of Mr. Garrick's friends, and by their aid he has been enabled to present to the public a collection which has been long enquired after, and which, from the care with which it has been formed, he trusts will not disgrace the memory of the author. Should the sources from whence the several pieces have been drawn be enumerated, he is certain that he should be allowed some merit from his industry, as almost every performance has been selected from a different publication, most of them very difficult to be procured, and some, from their scarcity, equal in value to manuscripts.

(Preface, pp. v-vi)

In establishing the texts of the poems in the present selection, the aim has been to take into account all relevant manuscripts, and at least all the printed versions of a poem which appeared during Garrick's lifetime. Many works which contain poems by Garrick but were published after his death have also been consulted — *The Poetical Works*, of course, but also the biographies of Garrick by his associates Thomas Davies and Arthur Murphy, the collected works of dramatists, where they print prologues and epilogues by Garrick, and various anthologies. In the textual notes, only the more interesting departures from the established text have been recorded. The textual notes do not attempt to duplicate the *Checklist of Verse by David Garrick* compiled by Mary E. Knapp. For a fuller account of extant manuscripts and printings of Garrick's verse, the *Checklist* should be consulted.

In presenting the poems, spelling and punctuation have been modernized and the use of italics and capitalization has generally been dispensed with wherever it would now be unorthodox. Exceptions to this are where the spelling attempts to reproduce dialectal speech, or where italics can increase clarity or indicate emphasis. The spelling " 'em" (for "them") has also been retained. In all quotations from manuscripts in the textual notes, however, an attempt has been made to give, as accurately as print will allow, an exact rendering of the original, including its spelling and punctuation. Where different manuscripts concur in a variant reading, and this reading does not occur in a printed text, the spelling, punctuation, etc. of the manuscript first mentioned have been reproduced.

SHORT TITLES AND ABBREVIATIONS

Where no other indication is given, London is to be understood as the place of publication of books.

AR	*The Annual Register*
BC	*Bath Chronicle*
Boaden	*The Private Correspondence of David Garrick* [ed. James Boaden], 1831-32
Boswell	*Boswell's Life of Johnson, together with Boswell's Journal of a Tour to the Hebrides and Johnson's Diary of a Journey into North Wales*, ed. George Birkbeck Hill, revised and enlarged by L.F. Powell, Oxford, 1934-50
Burgoyne's *Works*	*The Dramatic and Poetical Works of the late Lieut. Gen. J. Burgoyne*, 1808
CCM	*Court and City Magazine*
CS	*A Collection and Selection of English Prologues and Epilogues* [ed. Acton Frederick Griffith], 1779
CT	*The Court of Thespis; being a collection of the most admired prologues and epilogues that have appeared for many years*, 1769
Cumberland	*Memoirs of Richard Cumberland. Written by himself,* 2nd ed., 1807
Davies	Thomas Davies, *Memoirs of the Life of David Garrick,* 3rd. ed., 1781
Doran	John Doran, *Their Majesties' Servants. Annals of the English stage, from Thomas Betterton to Edmund Kean,* 1864
EE	*Elegant Extracts, or useful and entertaining pieces of poetry selected* [by V. Knox] *for the improvement of youth . . . .* 1796
ETW	*The Essence of Theatrical Wit: Being a Select Collection of the Best and Most Admired Prologues and Epilogues That Have Been Delivered from the Stage,* 1768
Folger	The Folger Shakespeare Library, Washington, D.C.
GA	*General Advertiser*
Genest	John Genest, *Some Account of the English Stage, from the Restoration in 1660 to 1830,* Bath, 1832
Gibbon's Journal	*Gibbon's Journal,* ed. D.M. Low, 1929
GIJ	*Gray's Inn Journal*
GM	*Gentleman's Magazine*
Goldsmith's *Works*	*Collected Works of Oliver Goldsmith,* ed. Arthur Friedman, Oxford, 1966

Huntington	Henry E. Huntington Library (Larpent Dramatic Collection), San Marino, California
Kearsley	George Kearsley (ed.), *The Poetical Works of David Garrick*, 1785; reprinted New York, 1968
LC	*London Chronicle*
LEP	*London Evening Post*
Letters	*The Letters of David Garrick*, ed. David M. Little and George M. Kahrl, Cambridge, Mass., 1963
Lichtenberg	Margaret L. Mare and W.H. Quarrell (eds.), *Lichtenberg's Visits to England*, Oxford, 1938
Ll EP	*Lloyd's Evening Post*
LM	*London Magazine*
Mallet's *Works*	*The Works of David Mallet*, 1759
MC	*Morning Chronicle*
MP	*Morning Post*
Murphy	Arthur Murphy, *The Life of David Garrick*, 1801
NFHW	*The New Foundling Hospital for Wit*, 1784
OPE	*Original Prologues and Epilogues and other Theatrical Pieces*, 1766
Osborn	The James Marshall and Marie-Louise Osborn Collection, the Beinecke Library, Yale University
PA	*Public Advertiser*
RM	*Royal Magazine*
SC	*The Spouter's Companion; or Theatrical Remembrancer. Containing a Select Collection of the most esteemed Prologues and Epilogues*, [1770?]
SJC	*St. James's Chronicle*
SM	*Scots Magazine*
TB	*The Theatrical Bouquet: containing an alphabetical arrangement of the prologues and epilogues, which have been published by distinguished wits*, 1780
TCM	*Town and Country Magazine*
UM	*Universal Magazine*
Victor	Benjamin Victor, *The History of the Theatres of London, from the Year 1760 to the Present Time*, 1771
WEP	*Whitehall Evening Post*
WM	*Westminster Magazine*
Yale	The Beinecke Rare Book and Manuscript Library, Yale University
Yearly Chronicle	*The Yearly Chronicle for MDCC, LXI. Or, a collection of the most interesting and striking essays, letters, etc. which appeared in the St. James's Chronicle for that year*, 1762

A CHRONOLOGY OF GARRICK'S LIFE.

1717	February 19th: David Garrick born at Hereford, where his father, Lieutenant Garrick, is on a recruiting mission. Returns with the family to their home at Lichfield.
1736	A student at Samuel Johnson's academy at Edial near Lichfield.
1737	Travels with Johnson to London.
1738-1741	In the wine trade in London, in association with his brother Peter at Lichfield.
1740	April 15th: his first play, *Lethe,* performed at Drury Lane.
1741	Plays the part of Harlequin at Goodman's Fields Theatre, when the actor Richard Yates is taken ill.
	Acts at Ipswich under an assumed name as a member of a summer company.
	October: engages as a professional actor at Goodman's Fields Theatre. Begins with the role of Richard III: ". . . the character of Richard was performed by a gentleman who never appeared before, whose reception was the most extraordinary and great that was ever known upon such an occasion." *London Daily Post and General Advertiser,* October 20th 1741.
1742	Plays during the summer at Smock Alley Theatre, Dublin.
1742-1745	A member of the Drury Lane company.
1745-1746	At the Smock Alley Theatre, Dublin.
1746-1747	A member of the Covent Garden company.
1747	April 9th: becomes partner of James Lacy in the management of Drury Lane Theatre.
1749	June 22nd: marries the Viennese dancer Eva Maria Veigel, "La Violette".
1754	Buys villa at Hampton.
1755	Samuel Johnson's *Dictionary of the English Language* published.
	November: "The Chinese Festival." Riots at Drury Lane over the employment of French dancers. Windows smashed at Garrick's house in Southampton Street.
1756-1763	War with France (the Seven Years' War).
1759	September 13th: defeat of the French at Quebec.
1761	March: *The Rosciad* by Charles Churchill published.
	September 22nd: coronation of George III.

1763	January 25th and 26th: rioting at Drury Lane over the decision to charge full price to latecomers at new productions (the Half-Price Riots).
1763-1765	The Garricks make the Grand Tour of Europe.
1764	August: Garrick contracts typhoid at Munich.
1765	.November 14th: returns to the stage as Benedick in *Much Ado About Nothing* — by Royal Command.
1769	September: the Shakespeare Jubilee at Stratford-on-Avon.
1776	Sells his share in Drury Lane to Richard Brinsley Sheridan and partners.
	June 10th: acts for the last time at Drury Lane.
1779	January 20th: dies at his house in the Adelphi.
1785	*The Poetical Works of David Garrick, Esquire*, edited by George Kearsley.

For those who wish to know more about Garrick's life, there are the following biographies:

Thomas Davies:	*Memoirs of the Life of David Garrick, Esq.*, 1780.
Arthur Murphy:	*The Life of David Garrick, Esq.*, 1801.
Percy Fitzgerald:	*The Life of David Garrick*, 1868; new and revised ed., 1899.
Joseph Knight:	*David Garrick*, 1894.
Mrs. Clement Parsons:	*Garrick and His Circle*, 1906.
Frank A. Hedgcock:	*David Garrick and His French Friends*, [1913].
Margaret Barton:	*Garrick*, 1948.
Carola Oman:	*David Garrick*, 1958.

A new biography of Garrick, by George M. Kahrl and George Winchester Stone, Jr., is to be published by the Southern Illinois University Press, Carbondale, in 1980.

1

UPON MR. QUIN'S SAYING THAT GARRICK WAS A NEW RELIGION, THAT WHITFIELD WAS FOLLOWED FOR A TIME, BUT THEY WOULD ALL COME TO CHURCH AGAIN (1741)

Pope Quin, who damns all churches but his own,
Cries out that heresy corrupts the town;
That Whitfield-Garrick has misled the age,
And taints the sound religion of the stage;
But soon they'll see their ignorance and sin,   5
And then they'll all come back to Church and Quin.
Thou great infallible, forbear to roar,
Thy bulls and errors are revered no more:
When doctrines meet with general approbation,
It is not heresy but reformation.   10

The text follows CCM (Aug. 1771) except that corrections made to this version in the Folger autograph (and copied in one of the two Folger transcripts) are incorporated. The text in CCM is verbally identical with that in Victor, GM (May 1779), Kearsley, and the Osborn transcript.

2   CCM *etc. read* Complains *for* Cries out.

5-6   CCM *etc. read:*

> Schism, he cries, has turned the nation's brain;
> But eyes will open, and to church again!

    When Garrick first went on the stage in 1741, James Quin (1693-1766) was the outstanding representative of the old school of declamatory actors. The two men remained rivals until Quin's retirement in 1751. Afterwards they became friends and Quin was a regular visitor of the Garricks at Hampton.

    On Quin, see also 16, 36, 38, 40.

2

EPILOGUE TO *THE LYING VALET* (1741)

spoken by Mr. Garrick

That I'm a lying rogue you all agree,
And yet look round the world and you will see
How many more, my betters, lie as fast as me.
Against this vice we all are ever railing,
And yet, so tempting is it, so prevailing,   5
You'll find but few without this useful failing.
Lady or Abigail, my Lord or Will,
The lie goes round and the ball's never still.
My lies were harmless, told to show my parts,
And not like those when tongues belie their hearts.   10
In all professions you will find this flaw,
And in the gravest, too, in Physic and in Law.
The gouty serjeant cries, with formal pause,
"Your plea is good, my friend, don't starve the cause."
But when my Lord decrees for t'other side,   15
Your costs of suit convince you that he lied.
A doctor comes, with formal wig and face,
First feels your pulse, then thinks, and knows your case.
"Your fever's slight, not dangerous, I assure you.
Keep warm, and *repetatur haustus*, sir, will cure you."   20
Around the bed, next day, his friends are crying.
The patient dies, the doctor's paid for lying.
The poet, willing to secure the pit,
Gives out his play has humour, taste and wit.
The cause comes on, and, while the judges try,   25
Each groan and catcall gives the bard the lie.
Now let us ask, pray, what the ladies do.
They too will fib a little *entre nous*.
"Lord!" says the prude, her face behind her fan,
"How can our sex have any joy in man?   30
As for my part, the best could ne'er deceive me,

And were the race extinct 'twould never grieve me.
Their sight is odious, but their touch — O Gad!
The thought of that's enough to drive one mad."
Thus rails at man the squeamish Lady Dainty,   35
Yet weds, at fifty-five, a rake of twenty.
In short, a beau's intrigues, a lover's sighs,
The courtier's promise, the rich widow's cries,
And patriot's zeal are seldom more than lies.
Sometimes you'll see a man belie his nation,   40
Nor to his country show the least relation.
For instance now —
A cleanly Dutchman, or a Frenchman grave,
A sober German, or a Spaniard brave,
An Englishman a coward or a slave.   45
Mine, though a fibbing, was an honest art;
I served my master, played a faithful part.
Rank me not, therefore, 'mongst the lying crew,
For though my tongue was false my heart was true.

The text follows that published with the 2nd ed. of the play (1743). The epilogue is not printed with the 1st ed.

Garrick's farce, *The Lying Valet*, was first performed at Goodman's Fields Theatre on November 30th 1741, with Garrick in the title role. The valet in question goes to great lengths of subterfuge and untruthfulness to conceal the poverty of his master from the rich young lady to whom he is engaged. On this epilogue, see Introduction, p. xxii.

3

EPILOGUE TO *REGULUS* (1744)

spoken by Mrs. Woffington

If one could credit what these poets tell us,
These Greeks and Romans were surprising fellows.
But when compared with heroes nowadays,
Who can believe one word our author says?

Tonight famed Regulus appeared before you,   5
Brimful of honour and his country's glory;
So fraught with virtue and with patriot zeal,
He laid down life to serve the public weal.
Bless me, was ever man so wildly frantic?
We have no patriots now are so romantic.   10
We've no state Quixotes as they had of yore;
Our patriots huff, 'tis true, and rant and roar,
And talk of this and that — but nothing more.

Their ladies too were formed with strange ingredients;
They loved their husbands and were all obedience: 15
And though their mates for many years would roam,
The constant doves would stay till they came home.
Martia, if what they say can gain belief,
For loss of husband almost died with grief;
And what is stranger still, they all agree   20
That Regulus was turned of sixty-three.
Would any modern lady break her heart
Because an aged spouse resolves to part?
Would she to thwart his will be so uncivil?
O no, the man might go to Carthage — or the devil!   25
What mighty stuff composed these sons of freedom!
The classics say (I'm told by those who read 'em)
That they were mortals of such wondrous merit,
That e'en when old they fought and loved with spirit.
Romans at sixty-three, as I'm alive,   30

4

Were better men than ours at thirty-five.
In short, if all that's said and wrote be true,
And they when old such mighty feats could do,
O Lord, they played the devil sure at twenty-two!

Thus far with trifling jests to please the age,   35
And to preserve the custom of the stage;
But now let serious, nobler thoughts impart
The warmest wishes to each English heart.
May every matron Martia's truth approve,
And every maid like constant Clelia love;   40
May every Decius find a faithful friend,
And every Corvus meet the villain's end;
May every Briton hold his country dear,
And Truth, not Party, every action steer;
May Regulus's conduct point the way,   45
And no false glitter lead our youths astray;
May every virtue be transplanted home,
And Britain boast the worth of ancient Rome.

The text follows that published with the play, 1744.

    Regulus, a tragedy by the actor William Havard, was first performed at Drury Lane, February 21st 1744, with Garrick as Regulus and Havard as Decius. It is based on a story told by Livy (*Periochae*, Book XVIII) and by Horace (*Odes*, III, v). Regulus was a distinguished Roman who had twice been consul. He was held as a prisoner-of-war in Carthage, but was allowed to accompany an embassy to Rome on the understanding that he would return if the Carthaginian peace proposals were not accepted. He himself urged the Roman senate not to accept them, and when he came back to Carthage he was tortured and killed. Martia is Regulus's wife, and Clelia his daughter whom he gives in marriage to Decius. Corvus, a Roman senator, is also in love with Clelia. In Act IV he is discovered to be a traitor in the pay of Carthage and he is subsequently put to death.

4

EPILOGUE TO *THE SUSPICIOUS HUSBAND* (1747)

spoken by Mrs. Pritchard

Though the young smarts, I see, begin to sneer,
And the old sinners cast a wicked leer,
Be not alarmed ye fair — you've nought to fear.
No wanton hint, no loose ambiguous sense
Shall flatter vicious taste at your expense.   5
Leaving for once these shameless arts in vogue,
We give a fable for the epilogue.

An ass there was, our author bid me say,
Who needs must write. He did — and wrote a play.
The parts were cast to various beasts and fowl,   10
Their stage a barn, the manager an owl.
The house was crammed at six with friends and foes —
Rakes, wits and critics, citizens and beaux.
These characters appeared in different shapes
Of tigers, foxes, horses, bulls and apes;   15
With others, too, of lower rank and station —
A perfect abstract of the brute creation.
Each as he felt marked out the author's faults,
And thus the connoisseurs expressed their thoughts.
The critic-curs first snarled "The rules are broke!   20
Time, place and action sacrificed to joke!"
The goats cried out 'twas formal, dull and chaste,
Not writ for beasts of gallantry and taste.
The horned cattle were in piteous taking
At fornication, rapes and cuckold-making.   25
The tigers swore he wanted fire and passion.
The apes condemned because it was the fashion.
The generous steeds allowed him proper merit,
Here marked his faults and there approved his spirit;
While brother bards brayed forth with usual spleen,   30
And, as they heard, exploded every scene.

6

When Reynard's thoughts were asked, the shrugging sage,
Famed for hypocrisy and worn with age,
Condemned the shameless licence of the stage.
At which the monkey skipped from box to box   35
And whispered round the judgement of the fox,
Abused the moderns, talked of Rome and Greece,
Bilked every box-keeper and damned the piece.

Now every fable has a moral to it.
Be churchman, statesman, anything but poet.   40
In law or physic quack in what you will.
Cant and grimace conceal the want of skill.
Secure in these his gravity may pass —
But here no artifice can hide the ass.

The text follows that published with the play, 1747.

    The Suspicious Husband is a comedy by Benjamin Hoadly, a distinguished
physician and a Fellow of the Royal Society. He is believed to have written
one or two other dramatic pieces, but these are no longer extant. *The
Suspicious Husband* was first performed at Covent Garden on February 12th
1747, with Garrick as Ranger, a young rake. This proved one of his most
successful and popular roles. Mrs. Pritchard, speaker of the epilogue, played
Clarinda, whose gay disposition leads Mr. Strickland, the suspicious husband,
into wholly unjustified misgivings about the moral character of his wife,
whose guest she is.

5

EPILOGUE AT THE OPENING OF DRURY LANE THEATRE, SEPTEMBER 15TH 1747

spoken by Mrs. Woffington

Sweet doings truly! We are finely fobbed!
And at one stroke of all our pleasures robbed!
No beaux behind the scenes! 'Tis innovation
Under the specious name of reformation!
Public complaint, forsooth, is made the puff —   5
Sense, order, decency and suchlike stuff.
But arguments like these are mere pretence —
The beaux, 'tis known, ne'er give the least offence,
Are men of chastest conduct and amazing sense.
Each actress now a locked-up nun must be,   10
And priestly managers must keep the key.
I know their selfish reasons — though they tell us,
While smarts and wits and other pretty fellows
Murmur their passions to our fluttering hearts,
The stage stands still and we neglect our parts.   15
But how mistaken in this silly notion!
We hear 'em talk without the least emotion.
Just as our tea we sip each tender strain,
Too weak to warm the heart or reach the brain.
If harmless, why are we debarred our rights?   20
Damsels distressed have ever found their knights.
Shall we, the Dulcineas of the stage,
In vain ask succour in this fighting age?
Will you choice spirits who direct the town
Suffer such impositions to go down?   25
Can it be thought this law will ever pass
While doors are only wood and windows glass?
Besides, our playhouse guards are passive men.
Strike without fear — they must not strike again.
Even Fribble here to draw his sword may venture,   30

May *cuse the creters*, beat his man and enter.
The jealous Moor not roars in louder strains
Than all our nymphs for loss of absent swains.
We had been happy, though the house had failed,
Masters and all, had not this scheme prevailed.   35
For ever now farewell the plumed beaux,
Who make ambition to consist in clothes.
Farewell coquetry and all green-room joys,
Ear-thrilling whispers, Deard's deluding toys,
Soul-melting flattery which even prudes can move,   40
Sighs, tears and all the circumstance of love,
Farewell!
But oh, ye dreadful critics, whose rude throats
Can make both players and masters change their notes —
'Tis in your power — you any lengths will run —   45
Help us, or else our occupation's gone!

The text follows that printed with Johnson's prologue for the occasion, by E. Cave for Cooper and Dodsley, 1747.

The 1747-48 season was the first of Garrick and Lacy's joint-management at Drury Lane. From the opening of the theatre on September 15th until October 17th, the following announcement appeared on the bills:

> As the admittance of persons behind the scenes has occasioned a general complaint on account of the frequent interruptions in the performance, 'tis hoped Gentlemen won't be offended that no money will be taken there for the future. (Genest, IV, 231-32)

The practice here referred to had been a nuisance for a long time, and often the progress of a play had been impeded by the presence of spectators on the stage. This practice, however, enabled a larger audience to be accommodated, and this was of advantage to actors on their benefit nights, when tiers of seats were set up on stage for the occasion. Opposition to reform, therefore, came from actors as well as from some sections of the public. It was not, in fact, until 1762, when the Drury Lane auditorium was enlarged to provide as many seats there as auditorium and stage together had previously provided, that there was any substantial abatement of the nuisance, and even then it was not complete.

Earlier in 1747, Garrick's farce *Miss in Her Teens* had been performed at Covent Garden. Lines 30-31 of this epilogue remind the audience of

Garrick's success in the role of the effeminate Fribble in that play. In particular, the scene is recalled where Fribble is prevailed on to draw his sword, having been assured that his adversary Flash is a coward. In line 31 (*"cuse the creters"*) Garrick reverts to the kind of speech affected by Fribble. Cf. the commentary on 32.

6

PROLOGUE AT THE OPENING OF DRURY LANE THEATRE, SEPTEMBER 8TH 1750

spoken by Mr. Garrick

As heroes, states and kingdoms rise and fall,
So, with the mighty to compare the small,
Through interest, whim, or, if you please, through fate,
We feel commotions in our mimic state.
The sock and buskin fly from stage to stage —   5
A year's alliance is with us an age.
And where's the wonder? All surprise must cease
When we reflect how interest or caprice
Makes real kings break articles of peace.
Strengthened with new allies, our foes prepare,   10
Cry "Havoc!" and let slip the dogs of war.
To shake our souls the papers of the day
Drew forth the adverse power in dread array —
A power might strike the boldest with dismay.
Yet fearless still we take the field with spirit,   15
Armed cap-a-pie in self-sufficient merit.
Our ladies, too, with souls and tongues untamed,
Fire up like Britons when the battle's named.
Each female heart pants for the glorious strife,
From Hamlet's mother to the Cobbler's wife.   20
Some few there are whom paltry passions guide,
Desert each day and fly from side to side.
Others, like Swiss, love fighting as their trade,
For, beat or beating, they must all be paid.

Sacred to Shakespeare was this spot designed,   25
To pierce the heart and humanize the mind.
But if an empty house, the actor's curse,
Shows us our Lears and Hamlets lose their force,
Unwilling, we must change the nobler scene,

And in our turn present you Harlequin;   30
Quit poets and set carpenters to work,
Show gaudy scenes or mount the vaulting Turk.
For though we actors, one and all, agree
Boldly to struggle for our vanity,
If want comes on, importance must retreat;   35
Our first great ruling passion is to eat.
To keep the field all methods we'll pursue,
The conflict glorious, for we fight for you.
And should we fail to gain the wished applause,
At least we're vanquished in a noble cause.   40

The text follows that published in GA *(Sept. 21, 1750) and in the Sept. 1750 issues of* GM *and* SM.

The 1750-51 season at Drury Lane, like that of 1747-48, began with *The Merchant of Venice*, but five of those who had taken part in the earlier production — including such distinguished performers as Spranger Barry, Charles Macklin and Mrs. Cibber — were now at the rival Covent Garden Theatre. So was Mrs. Woffington, speaker of the epilogue in 1747. Barry had actually broken his contract to go to Covent Garden — but then, Mrs. Ward had done the same thing, in the reverse direction, the season before. These defections — in which personal jealousies and disagreements had played a part — made the rivalry between the two theatres all the keener. Barry and Mrs. Cibber, who had played the leading roles in Garrick's 1748 production of *Romeo and Juliet*, now prepared to play them again at Covent Garden. Garrick countered by also reviving this play, with himself as Romeo and Miss Bellamy as Juliet. Both productions opened on September 28th 1750. That at Covent Garden ran for twelve nights; Garrick kept the play on for one night longer.

Pantomimes were much in favour at Covent Garden, whose manager, John Rich, was the greatest of English harlequins. Garrick, as he hints in his prologue, was ready to compete in this field as well. *Queen Mab*, "a new entertainment, in Italian grotesque characters", by Henry Woodward, who played the part of Harlequin, had the first of its forty-five performances on Boxing Day 1750.

With lines 25 ff. of this prologue, compare the following lines from the prologue which Johnson wrote for the opening of the Drury Lane season on September 15th 1747:

But who the coming changes can presage,
And mark the future periods of the stage?
....
Perhaps, where Lear has raved and Hamlet died,
On flying cars new sorcerers may ride.
Perhaps (for who can guess the effects of chance?)
Here Hunt may box, or Mahomet may dance.

Hard is his lot that, here by fortune placed,
Must watch the wild vicissitudes of taste;
With every meteor of caprice must play,
And chase the new-blown bubbles of the day.
Ah! let not censure term our fate our choice;
The stage but echoes back the public voice.
The drama's laws the drama's patrons give,
For we that live to please, must please to live.

7

OCCASIONAL PROLOGUE TO *THE ENGLISHMAN IN PARIS*
(1753)

spoken by Mr. Foote

The many various objects that amuse
These busy, curious times by way of news,
Are plays, elections, murders, lotteries, Jews.
All these compounded fly throughout the nation,
And set the whole in one great fermentation.   5
True British hearts the same high spirit show
Be they to damn a farce or fight a foe.
One day for liberty the Briton fires,
The next he flames for Canning or for Squires.
In like extremes your laughing humour flows: 10
Have ye not roared from pit to upper rows,
And all the jest was — what? — a fiddler's nose.
Pursue your mirth; each night the joke grows stronger,
For, as you fret the man, his nose looks longer.
Among the trifles which occasion prate   15
Even I sometimes am matter for debate.
Whene'er my faults or follies are the question
Each draws his wit out and begins dissection.
Sir Peter Primrose, smirking o'er his tea,
Sinks from himself and politics to me.   20
Papers, boy! — Here, sir! — Tam, what news today?
Foote, sir, is advertised. — What, run away?
No, sir, he acts this week at Drury Lane.
How's that (cries Feeble Grub) Foote come again?
I thought that fool had done his devil's dance.   25
Was not he hanged some months ago in France?
Up starts Machone and thus the room harangued:
'Tis true his friends gave out that he was hanged,
But, to be sure, 'twas all a hum, becase
I have seen him since and after such disgrace   30

No gentleman would dare to show his face.
To him replied a sneering bonny Scot:
You rasin reet my friend, haunged he was not,
But neither you nor I can tell how soon he'll gang to pot.
Thus each as fancy drives his wit displays. 35
Such is the tax each son of folly pays.
On this my scheme they many names bestow:
'Tis fame, 'tis pride, nay worse, the pocket's low.
I own I've pride, ambition, vanity,
And, what's more strange, perhaps you'll see, 40
Though not so great a portion of it, modesty.
For you I'll curb each self-sufficient thought,
And kiss the rod whene'er you point the fault.
Many my passions are though one my view:
They all concentre in the pleasing you. 45

The text follows that published in the Oct. 1753 issues of GM, SM *and* UM *and in* GIJ
No. 55 (Nov. 3, 1753).

The young Englishman in Paris in Samuel Foote's farce is called Buck, and
Foote himself played the role in the first Drury Lane performance of the
play on October 20th 1753. Foote had recently been in Paris and, as the
prologue reports (25-26), there had been a rumour that he had been hanged
there.

Foote (1720-77) was one of the most extraordinary characters of his
day. A great wit, he lived very extravagantly, and is said to have gone through
several fortunes, turning to the theatre whenever he needed money. As an
actor, his best performances were in plays of his own writing, which allowed
scope to his considerable talents as a mimic. In 1766 he lost a leg after being
thrown from a horse in the course of a practical joke in which the Duke of
York and Lord Mexborough were involved. The Duke of York then used his
influence to get him a royal patent for summer performances at the Little
Theatre in the Haymarket. Foote continued to act, with the help of an
artificial leg, even attempting — in the part of Sir Luke Limp in his comedy
The Lame Lover (1770) — to turn his incapacity to advantage.

8

EPILOGUE TO *VIRGINIA* (1754)

spoken by Mrs. Cibber

The poet's pen can, like a conjurer's wand,
Or kill, or raise his heroine at command:
And I shall, spirit-like, before I sink,
Not courteously enquire, but tell you what you think.
From top to bottom, I shall make you stare,   5
By hitting all your judgements to a hair.

And first with you above I shall begin —
                (To the upper gallery)
Good-natured souls, they're ready all to grin.
Though twelve-pence seat you there, so near the ceiling,
The folks below can't boast a better feeling.   10
No high-bred prudery in your region lurks,
You boldly laugh and cry as nature works.

Says John to Tom (ay — there they sit together,
As honest Britons as e'er trod on leather),
" 'Tween you and I, my friend, 'tis very *vild*,   15
That old Vergeenus should have stuck his child:
I would have hanged him for 't, had I been ruler,
And ducked that Apus too, by way of cooler."

Some maiden dames, who hold the middle floor,
                (To the middle gallery)
And fly from naughty man at forty-four,   20
With turned-up eyes applaud Virginia's 'scape,
And vow they'd do the same to shun a rape;
So very chaste, they live in constant fears,
And apprehension strengthens with their years.

Ye bucks, who from the pit your terrors send,   25
Yet love distressed damsels to befriend,
You think this tragic joke too far was carried,
And wish, to set all right, the maid had married.

16

You'd rather see (if so the fates had willed)
Ten wives be kind, than one poor virgin killed.   30

May I approach unto the boxes, pray,
And there search out a judgement on the play?
In vain, alas, I should attempt to find it!
Fine ladies see a play, but never mind it.
'Tis vulgar to be moved by acted passion,   35
Or form opinions, till they're fixed by fashion.

Our author hopes this fickle goddess, Mode,
With us will make, at least, nine days' abode;
To present pleasure he contracts his view,
And leaves his future fame to time and you.   40

The text follows that published with the play, 1754.

Virginia was first performed at Drury Lane on February 25th 1754.

The play is based mainly on a story told in Livy's history of Rome
(III, 58). Virginia, who was played by Mrs. Cibber, is desired by the powerful
and unscrupulous Appius. Her father, Virginius, played by Garrick, being
unable to save her from Appius by any other means, chooses to kill her with
his dagger rather than yield her up.

The author of this tragedy was the Rev. Samuel Crisp. In trying to
persuade Garrick to put on his play, he enlisted the support of powerful
friends, even getting William Pitt the elder to read and express his approval
of it. His final and successful stratagem is amusingly described by Murphy (I,
246-47). Crisp, he says,

> was related to, or patronized by, Lord Coventry. His Countess, the
> celebrated beauty of that day, as Garrick often related, drove to his house,
> and sent in word, that she had a moment's business. He went to the side of
> her carriage. "There, Mr. Garrick," said Lady Coventry, "I put into your
> hands a play, which the best judges tell me will do honour to you and the
> author." It was not necessary for her to say more: *Those eyes that tell us
> what the sun is made of*, as Dr. Young says in one of his tragedies, had all
> the power of persuasion, and even of command; Garrick obeyed, as if she
> had been a *tenth muse*, and prepared the play with the utmost dispatch.

Lady Coventry has another connection with this play. Tate Wilkinson
(*Original Anecdotes respecting the Stage and the Actors of the Old School,
with remarks on Mr. Murphy's "Life of Garrick"* [ca. 1805] , p. 17) says that
line 34 in Garrick's epilogue —

Fine ladies see a play, but never mind it —

was regarded as a satirical allusion to Lady Coventry.

9

AN ODE ON THE DEATH OF MR. PELHAM (1754)

Let others hail the rising sun,
I bow to that whose course is run,
    Which sets in endless night;
Whose rays benignant blessed this isle,
Made peaceful nature round us smile   5
    With calm but cheerful light.

No bounty past provokes my praise,
No future prospects prompt my lays,
    From real grief they flow;
I catch the alarm from Britain's fears,   10
My sorrows fall with Britain's tears,
    And join a nation's woe.

See, as you pass the crowded street,
Despondence clouds each face you meet,
    All their lost friend deplore.   15
You read in every pensive eye,
You hear in every broken sigh
    That Pelham is no more.

If thus each Briton be alarmed
Whom but his distant influence warmed,   20
    What grief their breasts must rend
Who, in his private virtues blessed,
By nature's dearest ties possessed
    The husband, father, friend.

What, mute ye bards — no mournful verse,   25
No chaplets to adorn his hearse,
    To crown the good and just?
Your flowers in warmer regions bloom,
You seek no pensions from the tomb,
    No laurels from the dust.   30

When power departed with his breath
The sons of flattery fled from death:
     Such insects swarm at noon.
Not for herself my muse is grieved,
She never asked, nor e'er received   35
     One ministerial boon.

Hath some peculiar strange offence
Against us armed Omnipotence,
     To check the nation's pride?
Behold the appointed punishment,   40
At length the vengeful bolt is sent;
     It fell when Pelham died.

Unchecked by shame, unawed by dread,
When vice triumphant rears her head,
     Vengeance can sleep no more;   45
The evil angel stalks at large,
The good submits, resigns his charge,
     And quits the unhallowed shore.

The same sad morn to Church and State
(So for our sins 'twas fixed by fate)   50
     A double stroke was given.
Black as the whirlwinds of the north
St. John's fell genius issued forth,
     And Pelham fled to heaven.

By angels watched in Eden's bowers,   55
Our parents passed their peaceful hours,
     Nor guilt nor pain they knew;
But on the day which ushered in
The hell-born train of mortal sin
     The heavenly guards withdrew.   60

Look down much-honoured shade below.
Still let thy pity aid our woe.
     Stretch out thy healing hand.
Resume those feelings which on earth
Proclaimed thy patriot love and worth   65
     And saved a sinking land.

Search with thy more than mortal eye
The breasts of all thy friends, descry
    What there has got possession.
See if thy unsuspecting heart   70
In some for truth mistook not art,
    For principle profession.

From these, the pests of human kind,
Whom royal bounty cannot bind,
    Protect our parent King.   75
Unmask their treachery to his sight,
Drag forth the vipers into light
    And crush them ere they sting.

If such his trust and honours share,
Again exert thy guardian care,   80
    Each venomed heart disclose.
On him, on him, our all depends.
Oh save him from his treacherous friends —
    He cannot fear his foes.

Who'er shall at the helm preside,   85
Still let thy prudence be his guide
    To stem the troubled wave;
But chiefly whisper in his ear
That George is open, just, sincere,
    And dares to scorn a knave.   90

No selfish views to oppress mankind,
No mad ambition fired thy mind,
    To purchase fame with blood;
Thy bosom glowed with purer heat,
Convinced that to be truly great   95
    Is only to be good.

To hear no lawless passion's call,
To serve thy King yet feel for all,
    Such was thy glorious plan.
Wisdom with generous love took part,   100
Together worked thy head and heart,
    The minister and man.

Unite ye kindred sons of worth,
Strangle bold faction in its birth,
    Be Britain's weal your view.   105
For this great end let all combine,
Let virtue link each fair design
    And Pelham live in you.

The text follows the 2nd ed. of the poem, 1754, for which, according to the "advertisement" at the end, the author "has altered some stanzas which were too hastily published in the first".

The Ode was written in 1754. Henry Pelham (1695?-1754) had been George II's prime minister since August 1743. He had shown himself well-disposed towards Garrick, who had acted as a go-between in the arrangements by which James Ralph, a journalist in the employ of political opponents, was bought off by the Pelham administration. Garrick's praise of Pelham, though fulsome, had some justification in fact. Even Horace Walpole, who was far from well-disposed towards Pelham, said of him that "he lived without abusing his power, and died poor" *(Memoirs of the Last Ten Years of the Reign of George the Second*, 1822, I, 322).

On March 6th 1754, the day of Pelham's death, there was published an edition of the works of the late deistically-inclined Henry St. John, Viscount Bolingbroke (see lines 49 ff.). The editor was the Scottish playwright David Mallet. Dr. Johnson was even more abusive than Garrick — of both author and editor. Bolingbroke was, he said, "a scoundrel and a coward: a scoundrel, for charging a blunderbuss against religion and morality; a coward, because he had no resolution to fire it off himself, but left half a crown to a beggarly Scotchman, to draw the trigger after his death!" (Boswell I, 268)

10

PROLOGUE TO *BARBAROSSA* (1754)

spoken by Mr. Garrick in the character of a country boy

    Measter! Measter!
Is not my measter here among you, pray?
Nay, speak — my measter wrote this fine new play.
The actor folks are making such a clatter.
They want the pro-log — I know nought o' the matter!   5
He must be there among you — look about:
A weezen, pale-faced man: do find him out.
Pray, measter, come, or all will fall to sheame.
Call Mister — hold — I must not tell his name.

Law, what a crowd is here! What noise and pother!   10
Fine lads and lasses one o' top o' t'other.
              (Pointing to the rows of pit & gallery)
I could for ever here with wonder geaze.
I ne'er saw church so full in all my days.
Your servunt, sirs. What do you laugh for, eh?
You donna take me sure for one o' th' play?   15
You should not flout an honest country lad.
You think me fool and I think you half mad.
You're all as strange as I and stranger too,
And if you laugh at me I'll laugh at you.
              (Laughing)
I donna like your London tricks, not I,
And since you've raised my blood I'll tell you why.
And if you wull, since now I am before ye,
For want of pro-log I'll relate my story.

I came from country here to try my fate,
And get a place among the rich and great.   25
But, troth, I'm sick o' the journey I ha' ta'en.
I like it not — would I were whoame again.

First in the city I took up my station,
And got a place with one of the Corporation,
A round big man — he eat a plaguy deal.   30
Zooks, he'd have beat five ploomen at a meal!
But long with him I could not make abode,
For, could you think't? He eat a great sea-toad!
It came from Indies — 'twas as big as me.
He called it "belly-patch" and "capapee".   35
Law, how I stared! I thought — who knows but I,
For want of monsters may be made a pie.
Rather than tarry here for bribe or gain,
I'll back to whoame and country fare again.

I left toad-eater; then I sarved a lord.   40
And there they promised but ne'er kept their word.
While 'mong the great this geaming work the trade is,
They mind no more poor servants than their ladies.

A lady next, who liked a smart young lad,
Hired me forthwith, but, troth, I thought her mad.   45
She turned the world top down, as I may say;
She changed the day to neet, the neet to day.
I stood one day with coach and did but stoop
To put the foot-board down, and with her hoop
She covered me all o'er. Where are you, lout?   50
Here, ma'am, says I, for heaven's sake let me out.
I was so sheamed with all her freakish ways,
She wore her gear so short, so low her stays —
Fine folks show all for nothing nowadays.

Now I'm the poet's man — I find with wits   55
There's nothing sartain — nay, we eat by fits.
Our meals, indeed, are slender — what of that?
There are but three on's — measter, I and cat.
Did you but see us all, as I'm a sinner,
You'd scarcely say which of the three is thinner.   60

My wages all depend on this night's piece;
But should you find that all our swans are geese,
E'feck! I'll trust no more to measter's brain,
But pack up all and whistle whoame again.

The text follows that published with the 2nd ed. of the play, 1755, which includes four lines (48-51) not found in the version published with the 1st ed. (also of 1755).

Barbarossa, by the Reverend John Brown, was first performed at Drury Lane on December 17th 1754.

Barbarossa has usurped the throne of Algiers after slaying the rightful king. He seeks also the death of the king's son, Selim, who has fled abroad, and he is determined to marry the widowed queen, by force if necessary. However, Selim returns in disguise to rally his supporters and the tyrant is overthrown. This is a ranting but lively play, which enjoyed great success. Garrick's performance as a country boy in the prologue was in sharp contrast to his role of Selim in the tragedy.

Brown had already made a name for himself with his *Essay on the Characteristics of Shaftesbury* (1751). *Barbarossa* was his first play, and, as the prologue makes clear, the playwright's name was at first concealed. He went on to write one other tragedy, *Athelstan* (see 14).

On this prologue, see Introduction, pp. xviii-xix.

11

EPILOGUE TO *BARBAROSSA* (1754)

spoken by Mr. Woodward in the character
of a fine gentleman

(Enter, speaking to the people without)
Pshaw, damn your epilogue and hold your tongue!
Shall we of rank be told what's right and wrong?
Had you ten epilogues you should not speak 'em,
Though he had writ 'em all in linguum Grecum.
I'll do't by all the gods! — you must excuse me —   5
Though author, actors, audience, all abuse me.

(To the audience)
Behold a gentleman, and that's enough!
Laugh if you please — I'll take a pinch of snuff.
I come to tell you — let it not surprise you —
That I'm a wit and worthy to advise you.   10
How could you suffer that same country booby,
That pro-logue speaking savage, that great looby,
To talk his nonsense? Give me leave to say
'Twas low, damned low — but save the fellow's play —
Let the poor devil eat, allow him that,   15
And give a meal to measter, mon and cat.
But why attack the fashions? Senseless rogue!
We have no joys but what result from vogue.
The mode should all control — nay, every passion,
Sense, appetite and all give way to fashion.   20
I hate as much as he a turtle-feast,
But till the present turtle rage has ceased,
I'd ride a hundred miles to make myself a beast.
I have no ears, yet operas I adore,
Always prepared to die, to sleep, no more.   25
The ladies too were carped at, and their dress;
He wants 'em all ruffed up like good Queen Bess.
They are, forsooth, too much exposed and free.

Were more exposed no ill effects I see,
For, more or less, 'tis all the same to me.   30
Poor gaming, too, was mauled among the rest,
That precious cordial to a high-life breast.
When thoughts arise I always game or drink;
An English gentleman should never think.
The reason's plain, which every soul might hit on —   35
What trims a Frenchman oversets a Briton.
In us reflection breeds a sober sadness
Which always ends in politics or madness.
I therefore now propose — by your command —
That tragedies no more shall cloud this land.   40
Send o'er your Shakespeares to the sons of France,
Let them grow grave, let us begin to dance.
Banish your gloomy scenes to foreign climes,
Reserve alone to bless these golden times
A farce or two — and Woodward's pantomimes.   45

*The text follows that published with the play, 1755. The opening stage direction is from
the 2nd ed. (1755). In the 1st ed. this reads* Enter — speaking without.

On this epilogue, see Introduction, pp. xvi and xix.

12

UPON JOHNSON'S DICTIONARY (1755)

Talk of war with a Briton, he'll boldly advance
That one English soldier will beat ten of France.
Would we alter the boast from the sword to the pen,
The odds are still greater, still greater our men.
In the deep mines of science though Frenchmen may toil,   5
Can their strength be compared to Locke, Newton and Boyle?
Let them rally their heroes, send forth all their powers,
Their verse-men and prose-men, then match 'em with ours.
First Milton and Shakespeare, like gods in the fight,
Have put their whole drama and epic to flight;   10
In satires, epistles and odes would they cope,
Their numbers retreat before Dryden and Pope;
And Johnson, well-armed, like a hero of yore,
Has beat forty French and will beat forty more.

The text follows that published in PA *(April 22, 1755),* LM *(April 1755) and* SM *(April 1755).*

      Samuel Johnson (1709-84), who had been Garrick's schoolmaster and had travelled to London with him from Lichfield in 1737, published his *Dictionary of the English Language* in 1755. This epigram was written to celebrate the occasion. It is reminiscent of a conversation recorded by Boswell (I, 186). Johnson had at first asserted that he would finish his dictionary in three years. When his friend Dr. Adams pointed out that it had taken the French Academy, with its forty members, forty years to compile its dictionary, Johnson replied: "Sir, thus it is. This is the proportion. Let me see; forty times forty is sixteen hundred. As three to sixteen hundred, so is the proportion of an Englishman to a Frenchman."

13

PROLOGUE TO *BRITANNIA* (1755)

spoken by Mr. Garrick in the character
of a sailor, fuddled and talking to himself

(He enters singing "How pleasant a sailor's life passes")
Well, if thou art, my boy, a little mellow,
A sailor half seas o'er 's a pretty fellow.
What cheer ho! Do I carry too much sail?
     (To the pit)
No, tight and trim, I scud before the gale.
     (He staggers forward, then stops)
But softly though — the vessel seems to heel.   5
Steady, my boy — she must not show her keel.
And now, thus ballasted, what course to steer?
Shall I again to sea and bang *Mounseer*?
Or stay on shore and toy with Sall and Sue?
Dost love 'em, boy? By this right hand I do!   10
A well-rigged girl is surely most inviting:
There's nothing better, faith, save flip and fighting.
For shall we sons of beef and freedom stoop,
Or lower our flag to slavery and soup?
What, shall these parleyvoos make such a racket,   15
And we not lend a hand to lace their jacket?
Still shall old England be your Frenchman's butt?
Whene'er he shuffles we should always cut.
I'll to 'em, faith — avast! — before I go
Have I not promised Sall to see the show?   20
(Pulls out a play bill)
From this same paper we shall understand
What work's tonight — I read your printed hand.
But, first, refresh a bit, for, faith, I need it.
I'll take one sugar-plum and then I'll read it.
     (Takes some tobacco)
(He reads the play bill of Zara, *which was acted that evening)*

At the The-atre Royal, Drury Lane,   25
will be presen-ta-ted a tragedy called
                    Sarah.
I'm glad 'tis *Sarah.* Then our Sal may see
Her namesake's tragedy, and as for me,
I'll sleep as sound as if I were at sea.   30
        To which will be added a new masque.
Zounds! Why a masque? We sailors hate grimaces.
Above board all, we scorn to hide our faces.
But what is here so very large and plain?
Bri-tan-nia — oh Britannia! — good again.   35
Huzza, boys! By the Royal George I swear,
Tom coxon and the crew shall straight be there.
All free-born souls must take Bri-tan-nia's part,
And give her three round cheers, with hand and heart.
(Going off, he stops)
I wish you landmen, though, would leave your tricks,   40
Your factions, parties and damned politics,
And, like us honest tars, drink, fight and sing,
True to yourselves, your country and your king.

The text follows that printed in Mallet's Works, *1759. Garrick and Mallet are said to have collaborated in the writing of this prologue. GM (May 1755) gives a slightly different version of the prologue and has a footnote stating that "the copy inserted here, which was taken in short hand, as it was spoke on the third night, and corrected the fourth, differs from the copy that has been lately printed and prefixed to the Masque". This statement is reiterated in SM (May 1755) and in Kearsley, although their versions differ slightly from each other and neither is identical with the GM text. I have been unable to trace any edition of the masque, such as GM etc. refer to, which includes the prologue. The 1755 ed., printed for A. Millar, does not do so.*

David Mallet's very patriotic masque *Britannia* was first performed at Drury Lane on May 9th 1755.

Feeling against the French was mounting throughout 1755, and naval actions against them began in June. Garrick's performance as a drunken sailor was extremely popular, and the prologue was several times called for when *Britannia* was not on the bill. The text of the song with which Garrick made his entry can be found in C.H. Firth's *Naval Songs and Ballads* (1908), pp. 164-65. As its first stanza illustrates, the song expresses sentiments about "faction" and the British tar similar to those with which the prologue concludes:

How pleasant a sailor's life passes,
Who roams o'er the watery main!
No treasure he ever amasses,
But cheerfully spends all his gain.
We're strangers to party and faction,
To honour and honesty true,
And would not commit a base action
For power or profit in view.

On this prologue, see Introduction, p. xx.

14

EPILOGUE TO *ATHELSTAN* (1756)

spoken by Mrs. Cibber

To speak ten words, again I've fetched my breath:
The tongue of woman struggles hard with death.
Ten words! Will that suffice? Ten words — no more.
We always give a thousand to the score.

What can provoke these wits their time to waste,   5
To please that fickle, fleeting thing called "taste"?
It mocks all search, for substance has it none;
Like Hamlet's ghost, 'tis here, 'tis there, 'tis gone.
How very few about the stage agree.
As men with different eyes a beauty see,   10
So judge they of that stately dame Queen Tragedy.

The Greek-read critic as his mistress holds her,
And having little love, for trifles scolds her:
Excuses want of spirit, beauty, grace,
But ne'er forgives her failing time and place.   15
How do our sex of taste in judgement vary?
Miss Bell adores what's loathed by Lady Mary.
The first, in tenderness a very dove,
Melts like the feathered snow at Juliet's love,
Then, sighing, turns to Romeo by her side,   20
"Can you believe that men for love have died?"
Her Ladyship, who vaults the courser's back,
Leaps the barred gate and calls you Tom and Jack,
Detests these whinings like a true virago.
She's all for daggers! Blood! Blood! Blood! Iago!   25
A third, whose heart defies all perturbations,
Yet dies for triumphs, funerals, coronations,
Ne'er asks which tragedies succeed or fail,
But whose procession has the longest tail.
The youths to whom France gives a new belief,   30
Who look with horror on a rump of beef,

On Shakespeare's plays with shrugged-up shoulders stare:
"These plays? They're bloody murders! *O barbare!*
And yet the man has merit — *entre nous* —
He'd been damned clever had he read Bossu."   35
"Shakespeare read French!" roars out a surly cit:
"When Shakespeare wrote our valour matched our wit.
Had Britons then been fops Queen Bess had hanged 'em.
Those days they never read the French — they banged 'em."

If taste evaporates by too high breeding,   40
And eke is overlaid by too deep reading,
Lest, then, in search of this you lose your feeling
And barter native sense in foreign dealing,
Be this neglected truth to Britons known:
No tastes, no modes become you but your own.   45

The text follows that published with the play, 1756.

Athelstan, a tragedy by the Reverend John Brown, was first performed
at Drury Lane on February 27th 1756.

Athelstan, Duke of Mercia, played by Garrick, is a traitor who has
assisted the Danes in the capture of London. Thyra, played by Mrs. Cibber, is
a captive whom the Danish commander, Gothmund, plans to ravish. Athelstan
discovers that Thyra is his lost daughter. Intending to kill Gothmund, he
mistakenly stabs and kills Thyra instead, and dies of a broken heart.

At a time when a French invasion seemed likely, Brown's play was a
terrible warning to any potential collaborators. The concluding lines of the
prologue, written by Brown himself, emphasized this:

> Treason, attend! — here view the rebel's fate;
> Nor hope thy arm can shake a free-born state;
> See blood and horror end what guilt began;
> And tremble at *thy* woes in *Athelstan*.

> (Printed with the play, 1756)

15

VERSES WRITTEN FOR HOGARTH'S PRINTS OF FRANCE AND ENGLAND (1756)

Plate I

With lantern jaws and croaking gut,
See how the half-starved Frenchmen strut
    And call us English dogs.
But soon we'll teach these bragging foes
That beef and beer give heavier blows   5
    Than soup and roasted frogs.

The priests, inflamed with righteous hopes,
Prepare their axes, wheels and ropes,
    To bend the stiff-necked sinner.
But should they sink in coming over,   10
Old Nick may fish 'twixt France and Dover,
    And catch a glorious dinner.

Plate II

See John the soldier, Jack the tar,
With sword and pistol armed for war,
    Should Monsieur dare come here.
The hungry slaves have smelt our food,
They long to taste our flesh and blood,   5
    Old England's beef and beer.

Britons to arms and let 'em come!
Be you but Britons still, strike home,
    And lion-like attack 'em.
No power can stand the deadly stroke   10
That's given from hands and hearts of oak,
    With liberty to back 'em.

The text follows that published with the prints, 1756.

William Hogarth (1697-1764), the painter and engraver, was a close friend of Garrick. The prints referred to, with Garrick's verses underneath, were first published in March 1756, when a French invasion seemed imminent.

Of the two plates, the first represents a scene on the French coast, where troops are embarking for an invasion of England. In front of an inn which advertises vegetable soup only, a French officer roasts frogs on his sword and points to a flag which bears the caption (in French): "Vengeance and the good beer and good beef of England". There is also a monk testing the sharpness of an axe, and on a sledge are various objects suggestive of Roman Catholicism and the Inquisition.

The second plate, set in England, includes a grenadier painting a caricature of the King of France on an inn wall, his sword balanced meanwhile on a round of beef, and a sailor with his pistol on top of a large tankard of beer. A youth who is being measured by a recruiting sergeant and who stands on tiptoe to increase his height was said to be a drawing of Garrick.

When invasion again seemed imminent in September 1759, the prints were republished. The advertisement in the *London Chronicle* (Sept. 20th-22nd 1759) says they are "Proper to be stuck up in public places, both in town and country, at this juncture".

See *Hogarth's Graphic Works*, ed. Ronald Paulson, New Haven and London, 1965, volume II, plates 222 and 223.

16

ON MR. QUIN'S SENDING FOR HIS SPECTACLES WHICH
HE LEFT AT MY HOUSE (1756)

He that is robbed, not wanting what is stolen,
Let him not know't, and he's not robbed at all.
Othello.

From Shakespeare's law there's no appeal
To show what is, what not to steal.
To keep the spectacles you left,
As you must want them, would be theft.
Your sight, alas, the worse for wear,   5
Your spectacles you cannot spare.
But when, my friend, you leave behind
Strong tokens of a vigorous mind:
That coin, which never false or light,
That sterling wit you pay at sight;   10
That humour trolling from your tongue,
So bold, emphatical and strong;
That various whim, that social glee,
The quick enlivening repartee,
Jack Falstaff's rich variety;   15
Such, when you leave, to you unknown,
Without a theft I'll make my own.
You can't be robbed, yourself must grant,
Of what you neither miss nor want.

The text follows that published in SJC *(Sept. 24-26, 1765),* LM *(Nov. 1765),* SM *(Dec. 1765) and the anonymous* Life of Mr. James Quin, Comedian, *1766. The two Folger transcripts, both with corrections in Garrick's hand, represent earlier stages of composition. One of them is dated August 1756.*

On Quin, see also 1, 36, 38, 40.

17

THE BEER-DRINKING BRITON (1756)

Ye true honest Britons who love your own land,
Whose sires were so brave, so victorious and free,
Who always beat France when they took her in hand,
Come join honest Britons in chorus with me.

Let us sing our own treasures, old England's good cheer,   5
The profits and pleasures of stout British beer.
Your wine-tippling, dram-sipping fellows retreat,
But your beer-drinking Britons can never be beat.

The French with their vineyards are meagre and pale;
They drink of the squeezing of half-ripened fruit.   10
But we, who have hop grounds to mellow our ale,
Are rosy and plump and have freedom to boot.

Let us sing our own treasures etc.

Should the French dare invade us, thus armed with our poles,
We'll bang their bare ribs, make their lantern-jaws ring.
For your beef-eating, beer-drinking Britons are souls   15
Who will shed their last drop for their country and king.

Let us sing our own treasures etc.

*The text follows that published with Thomas Arne's music in 1756, except that the
repetitions occasioned by the music are ignored.*

Garrick contributed this song to Henry Woodward's pantomime
Harlequin Mercury, first performed at Drury Lane on December 27th, 1756.
The singer was John Beard.

18

EPIGRAM WRITTEN SOON AFTER DR. HILL'S FARCE
THE ROUT WAS ACTED (1758)

For physic and farces his equal there scarce is;
His farces are physic, his physic a farce is.

The text is as found in NFHW, *Kearsley, the Folger autograph and the two Folger transcripts, except that in* NFHW *and Kearsley it is set out in four lines.*

John Hill (1716?-75) was a man of many talents, who was widely known as an apothecary. The *Public Advertiser* of February 26th 1766 carries an advertisement for his "Tincture of Sage", priced at three shillings a bottle, which, amongst its many other virtues, "continues health and spirits to the extreme of life, preserves the faculties and memory, warms the heart, and strengthens the stomach".

Hill was a very vain man. He styled himself Sir John Hill after the King of Sweden gave him the Order of St. Vasa in recognition of his botanical work. When his vanity was offended he usually responded with scurrilous abuse. He published two attacks on the Royal Society after failing in his efforts to become a Fellow. At least one of his victims gave him a public beating. The actor Henry Woodward would have liked to do the same when Hill abused him in the "The Inspector", the letter he contributed to the *London Daily Advertiser*, but Hill was not to be found. Woodward contented himself with publishing *A Letter from Henry Woodward, Comedian, the meanest of all characters (see Inspector No. 524); to Dr. John Hill, Inspector-General of Great Britain, the greatest of all characters (see all the Inspectors)*, 1752.

Garrick's quarrel with Hill had to do with Hill's farce *The Rout*, performed at Drury Lane on 20th and 21st December 1758. The failure of his play led to Hill's reviling the Drury Lane management in the press. Garrick says (*Letters*, No. 222) that he composed his epigram extempore, as a suggested motto for a portrait of Hill.

On Hill, see also 19 and 20.

19

UPON THE FARCE OF *THE ROUT* WRITTEN
BY A PERSON OF HONOUR (1758)

Says a friend to the Doctor, "Pray give it about
That this farce is not yours, or the house will not fill;
What had come of your *nerves*, or your *pox*, or your *gout*,
Had these embryos crawled forth as begot by John Hill?
Let your Muse, as your pamphlets, come forth, I advise ye,   5
Like a goddess of old with a cloud cast upon her."
"You're right," quoth the Doctor, "and more to disguise me,
I'll give myself out for a Person of Honour."

*Folger has a transcript of this epigram with revisions in Garrick's hand affecting lines 2
and 4. In each case, Garrick gives two revision, leaving both standing, as if he had not yet
finally chosen between them. The present text adopts one set of revisions; the other is
noted below. The epigram as printed in* LC *(Jan. 16–18, 1759) coincides verbally with
the transcript before it was revised.*

2   LC *reads* you'll miss of the pelf *for* the house will not fill.
        Transcript has alternative revision at foot of page:
        That the Farce is not Y^{rs} or they'll give you Y^{r} due.

4   LC *reads* yourself *for* John Hill.
        Transcript has alternative revision at foot of page:
        Had the Embrios crawld forth as Begotten by You.

John Hill's authorship of *The Rout* (see 18) was not made public until
the second performance, which was for his benefit. The first performance was
in aid of the General Lying-In Hospital, and the farce was announced as being
written by "a Person of Honour".

Hill made use of various assumed names when writing of such diseases
as those mentioned in line 3 — so says a footnote in both *The London
Chronicle* and the Folger transcript.

On this epigram, and on Charles Churchill's account of Hill in *The
Rosciad*, see Introduction, pp. xiii-xiv.

20

TO DR. HILL UPON HIS PETITION OF *I* AND *U* TO
MR. GARRICK (1759)

If 'tis true, as you say, that I've injured a letter,
I'll change my note soon and I hope for the better;
May the just rights of letters, as well as of men,
Hereafter be fixed by the tongue and the pen;
Most devoutly I wish that they both have their due,
And that *I* may be never mistaken for *U*.

The text follows the fair copy of the epigram in Garrick's hand in the possession of the New York Public Library. This departs from the version published in AR *(1759) and* UM *(Oct. 1776) only at line 3.*

3.   AR, UM *read* right *for* rights.

On Dr. John Hill, see 18 and 19.

This epigram is a reply to Hill's pamphlet *To David Garrick, Esq.: the petition of* I *in behalf of herself and her sisters* (1759), which accuses Garrick of pronouncing the letter *i* as if it were *u*. Hill asserts, indeed, that the "indelicate and indeterminate sound *u*" has, in Garrick's pronunciation, "taken the place of most of the vowels and dipthongs" (p. 9).

21

EPILOGUE TO *THE ORPHAN OF CHINA* (1759)

spoken by Mrs. Yates

Through five long acts I've wore my sighing face,
Confined by critic laws to time and place;
Yet, that once done, I ramble as I please,
Cry "London hoy!" and whisk o'er land and seas —
Ladies, excuse my dress — 'tis true Chinese.   5
Thus, quit of husband, death and tragic strain,
Let us enjoy our dear small talk again.

How could this bard successful hope to prove?
So many heroes — and not one in love!
No suitor here to talk of flames that thrill;   10
To say the civil thing — "Your eyes so kill!"
No ravisher to force us to our will.
You've seen their eastern virtues, patriot passions,
And now for something of their taste and fashions.
"O Lord! that's charming," cries my Lady Fidget,   15
"I long to know it. Do the creatures visit?
Dear Mrs. Yates, do tell us. Well, how is it?"

First, as to beauty — set your hearts at rest —
They're all broad foreheads, and pig's eyes at best.
And then they lead such strange, such formal lives —   20
A little more at home than English wives.
Lest the poor things should roam and prove untrue,
They all are crippled in the tiny shoe.
A hopeful scheme to keep a wife from madding!
We pinch our feet and yet are ever gadding.   25
Then they've no cards, no routs, ne'er take their fling,
And pin money is an unheard-of thing.
Then how d'ye think they write? You'll ne'er divine —
From top to bottom down in one straight line.   *(Mimics.)*
We, ladies, when our flames we cannot smother,   30

Write letters from one corner to another.   *(Mimics.)*

One mode there is in which both climes agree.
I scarce can tell — 'mongst friends then let it be —
The creatures love to cheat as well as we.

But bless my wits! I've quite forgot the bard.   35
A civil soul, by me he sends this card —
Presents respects to every lady here —
Hopes for the honour of a single tear.
The critics then will throw their dirt in vain;
One drop from you will wash out every stain.   40
Acquaints you (now the man is past his fright)
He holds his rout, and here he keeps his night.
Assures you all a welcome kind and hearty;
The ladies shall play crowns — and there's the shilling party.
                    (Points to the upper gallery.)

The text follows that published with the play, 1759.

Arthur Murphy's *The Orphan of China* was first performed at Drury Lane on April 21st 1759. Adapted from Voltaire's *L'Orphelin de la Chine*, which had been performed in Paris in 1755, it deals with the attempts of Zamti and his wife Mandane to save Zaphimri, the one member of the Chinese royal family who has not fallen victim to the invading Tartars. In Voltaire's play, Zaphimri is an infant, but Murphy makes him a young man who finally fights with and slays the Tartar Emperor, Timurkan. Mrs. Yates, speaker of the epilogue, played the part of Mandane.

It took Murphy a long time to persuade Garrick to stage his play. Garrick was reluctant not only because of his reservations about the play, but also because he had a prior arrangement with another dramatist, John Hawkesworth, that he should prepare a version of Voltaire's play. Hawkesworth's version, however, was not forthcoming. Murphy's script went back and forward between himself and Garrick, with Garrick offering fresh criticisms each time; it was offered by Murphy to Covent Garden, and then returned to Garrick; influential people were prevailed on to praise the play in Garrick's hearing; it went finally to an arbiter, William Whitehead, the Poet Laureate, who also made adverse criticisms, but, on the whole, pronounced in its favour. When, at last, Garrick had accepted the play, Mrs. Cibber, who was to have played Mandane, fell ill, and he wanted to postpone the opening. Murphy, however, persuaded him to let Mrs. Yates have the part instead.

In spite of Garrick's doubts, the play ran for nine nights and was well received. Garrick was very moving in the part of Zamti, and Mrs. Yates, as Mandane, established her reputation as a tragic actress.

22

HEART OF OAK (1759)

Come cheer up my lads, 'tis to glory we steer,
To add something more to this wonderful year.
To honour we call you, not press you like slaves,
For who are so free as we sons of the waves?

    Chorus.
Heart of oak are our ships, heart of oak are our men;   5
We always are ready — steady, boys, steady —
We'll fight and we'll conquer again and again.

We ne'er see our foes but we wish 'em to stay.
They never see us but they wish us away.
If they run, why, we follow and run 'em ashore,   10
For if they won't fight us, we cannot do more.

Heart of oak etc.

They swear they'll invade us, these terrible foes.
They frighten our women, our children and beaux.
But should their flat-bottoms in darkness get o'er,
Still Britons they'll find to receive them on shore.   15

Heart of oak etc.

We'll still make 'em run and we'll still make 'em sweat,
In spite of the devil and *Brussels Gazette.*
Then cheer up my lads, with one heart let us sing
Our soldiers, our sailors, our statesmen and king.

Heart of oak etc.

The text follows that published with Boyce's music in 1759? and 1765?

This well-known song comes from *Harlequin's Invasion*, a pantomime or "Christmas Gambol" by David Garrick, first performed at Drury Lane on December 31st 1759, in which it was sung by Samuel Champness. In this pantomime, Harlequin and his followers invade the domain of Shakespeare, but they are defeated and King Shakespeare restored. The music for the pantomime was composed by William Boyce.

1759, *this wonderful year* (line 2) had seen a succession of victories for British forces in various parts of the world, culminating in the defeat of the French at Quebec on September 13th.

James Boswell, in his *Account of Corsica* (1768), tells how he sang this song to his Corsican hosts:

> I translated it into Italian for them, and never did I see men so delighted with a song as the Corsicans were with Hearts of Oak. "Cuore di quercia", cried they, "bravo, Inglese!" It was quite a joyous riot. I fancied all my chorus of Corsicans aboard the British fleet.
>
> *(Boswell on the Grand Tour: Italy, Corsica and France, 1765-1766*, ed. F. Brady and F.A. Pottle, London, 1955, pp. 185-86).

Boswell's entitling the song "Hearts of Oak" is not surprising. Garrick himself uses this title in a letter to Boswell (*Letters,* No. 493) and also in his epilogue to *All in the Wrong* (31, line 30). "Hearts of oak" and "heart of oak" were both phrases that had been in use for a long time. *Stevenson's Book of Quotations* (9th ed., 1964, p. 562) gives instances from the seventeenth century:

> Here is a dozen yonkers that have hearts of oak at fourscore years (*Old Mag of Herefordshire,* 1609);
>
> He was heart of oak; he wore like iron
> (Walker, *Paroemiologia,* 24, 1672).

Garrick had used the phrase "hearts of oak" in earlier pieces, e.g. to refer to the occupants of the upper gallery, in his prologue to *Florizel and Perdita,* 1756 (Kearsley, I, 140). Cf. also his verses written to accompany Hogarth's prints (15, *II,* line 11).

23

SONG sung by Zaida in *THE ENCHANTER* (1760)

Whate'er you say, whate'er you do,
    My heart shall still be fixed and true.
The vicious bosom love deforms
    And rages there in gusts and storms,
But love with us a constant gale,   5
Just swells the sea and fills the sail:
Neither of winds or waves the sport,
We rule the helm and gain the port.

24

SONG sung by Lyssa in _THE ENCHANTER_ (1760)

When youthful charms
Fly pleasure's arms
Kind nature's gifts are vain;
We should not save
What nature gave,
But kindly give again.

Though scorn and pride
Our wishes hide
And though the tongue says "Nay",
The honest heart
Takes pleasure's part,
Denying all we say.

The birds in spring
Will sport and sing
And revel through the grove;
And shall not we,
As blithe and free,
With them rejoice and love?

Let love and joy
Our spring employ,
Kind nature's law fulfil;
Then sport and play
Now whilst we may,
We cannot when we will.

25

DUET FROM *THE ENCHANTER* (1760)

Lyssa:

Would you taste the sweets of love?
Ever change and ever rove,
    Fly at pleasure and away.
Love's the cup of bliss and woe,
Nectar if you taste and go,
    Poison if you stay.

Zaida:

Would you taste the sweets of love?
Never change and never rove,
    Fly from pleasures that betray.
Love's the cup of bliss and woe,
Poison if you taste and go,
    Nectar if you stay.

The texts of the three songs from The Enchanter *are as published with the play, 1760.*

The Enchanter, or Love and Magic, a musical entertainment by David Garrick, with music by John Christopher Smith, was first performed at Drury Lane on December 13th 1760.

Moroc is an Enchanter who has made Zaida his captive and seeks to seduce her by the pleasures he offers. She, however, remains faithful to her old love, Zoreb, and will not yield. Lyssa is a female spirit in the employ of Moroc. Zaida and Zoreb are reunited when Kaliel, another of Moroc's attendant spirits, seizes his master's wand and overthrows him.

Miss Young — not to be confused with the speaker of the epilogue to *The Runaway* (52) — played Lyssa, and Mrs. Vincent played Zaida.

26

PROLOGUE TO *THE DESERT ISLAND* (1760)

spoken by Mr. Garrick in the character of a drunken poet

(Enter speaking to those behind the scenes)
All, all shall out — all that I know and feel;
I will, by heaven, to higher powers appeal!
Behold a bard — no author of tonight —
No, no — they can't say that, with all their spite.
Ay, you may frown *(Looking behind the scenes)*.
      I'm at you, great and small —   5
Your poet, players, managers and all.
These fools within here swear that I'm in liquor.
My passion warms me, makes my utterance thicker.
I totter too, but that's the gout and pain —
French wines and living high have been my bane.   10
From all temptations now I wisely steer me,
Nor will I suffer one fine woman near me.
And this I sacrifice to give you pleasure —
For you I've coined my brains, and here's the treasure.
      (Pulls out a manuscript.)
A treasure this of profit and delight —   15
And all thrown by for this damned stuff tonight.
This is a play would water every eye.
If I but look upon't, it makes me cry.
This play would tears from blood-stained soldiers draw,
And melt the bowels of hard-hearted Law;   20
Would fore and aft the storm-proof sailor rake,
Keep turtle-eating aldermen awake;
Would the cold blood of ancient maidens thrill,
And make even pretty younger tongues lie still.
This play not even managers would refuse,   25
Had heaven but given 'em any brains to choose.
      (Puts up his manuscript.)
Your bard tonight, bred in the ancient school,
Designs and measures all by critic rule.

'Mongst friends — it goes no farther — he's a fool.
So very classic and so very dull,   30
His *Desert Island* is his own dear skull:
No soul to make the playhouse ring and rattle,
No trumpets, thunder, ranting, storms or battle,
But all your fine poetic prittle-prattle.
The plot is this: a lady's cast away —   35
Long before the beginning of the play—
And they are taken by a fisherman,
The lady and the child — 'tis Bayes's plan —
So on he blunders — he's an Irishman!
'Tis all alike — his comic stuff I mean —   40
I hate all humour — it gives me the spleen;
So damn 'em both with all my heart, unsight, unseen.
But should you ruin him, still I'm undone —
I've tried all ways to bring my phoenix on.
                              (Showing his play again.)
Flatter I can with any of our tribe,   45
Can cut and slash — indeed I cannot bribe.
What must I do then — beg you to subscribe?
Be kind, ye boxes, galleries and pit,
'Tis but a crown apiece for all this wit —
All sterling wit — to puff myself I hate —   50
You'll ne'er supply your wants at such a rate.
'Tis worth your money — I would scorn to wrong ye.
You smile consent — I'll send my hat among ye.
                              (Going, he returns.)
So much beyond all praise your bounties swell,
Not my own tongue my gra - ti - tude can tell —   55
A little flattery sometimes does well.
                              (Staggers off.)

The text follows that published with the play, 1760.

The *Desert Island*, by Arthur Murphy, was first performed at Drury Lane on January 24th 1760. The play, as the prologue indicates, is about a mother and daughter stranded on a desert island. The husband comes in search of them and is eventually reunited with his wife, while his companion marries the daughter.

Garrick was only too familiar with the kind of character he portrays in this prologue — the playwright who, when his play is rejected, maligns the manager's judgement. Murphy had himself been troublesome in this way in the past. He was annoyed now because Garrick was putting on his two new plays, *The Desert Island* and *The Way to Keep Him*, both on the same evening, and was himself only taking part in the latter.

27

EPILOGUE TO *POLLY HONEYCOMBE* (1760)

spoken by Miss Pope

(Enter, as Polly, laughing) Ha, ha, ha!
My poor papa 's in woeful agitation,
While I, the cause, feel here *(striking her bosom)*
        no palpitation.
We girls of reading and superior notions,
Who from the fountainhead drink love's sweet potions,
Pity our parents when such passion blinds 'em;   5
One hears the good folks rave — one never minds 'em.
Till these dear books infused their soft ingredients,
Ashamed and fearful, I was all obedience.
Then my good father did not storm in vain —
I blushed and cried "I'll ne'er do so again."   10
But now no bugbears can my spirit tame,
I've conquered fear, and almost conquered shame;
So much these dear instructors change and win us,
Without their light we ne'er should know what 's in us.
Here we at once supply our childish wants —   15
Novels are hotbeds for your forward plants.
Not only sentiments refine the soul,
But hence we learn to be the smart and droll:
Each awkward circumstance for laughter serves,
From nurse's nonsense to my mother's nerves.   20

Though parents tell us that our genius lies
In mending linen and in making pies,
I set such formal precepts at defiance
That preach up prudence, neatness, and compliance,
Leap these old bounds, and boldly set the pattern   25
To be a wit, philosopher, and slattern.

O did all maids and wives my spirit feel,
We'd make this topsy-turvy world to reel!
Let us to arms — our fathers, husbands, dare!

Novels will teach us all the art of war.   30
Our tongues will serve for trumpet and for drum.
I'll be your leader — General Honeycombe!

Too long has human nature gone astray.
Daughters should govern, parents should obey.
Man should submit the moment that he weds,   35
And hearts of oak should yield to wiser heads.
I see you smile, bold Britons, but 'tis true:
Beat you the French — but let your wives beat you.

The text follows that published with the play, 1760.

Polly Honeycombe, a farce by George Colman the elder, was first performed at Drury Lane on December 5th 1760.

The previous ten years or so had seen a great outpouring of novels, many of them novels of sentiment in the manner of Samuel Richardson (1689-1761), and Polly Honeycombe (who was played by Miss Pope) has cast herself in the part of a Richardson heroine.

Polly's father wants her to marry Ledger, but she, her head full of the novels she has been reading, falls in love with Scribble and elopes with him, not perceiving that he is only interested in her fortune. She is brought back and Scribble is sent packing, but Ledger decides she is no wife for him. In his curtain line, Polly's father concludes that "a man might as well turn his daughter loose in Covent Garden, as trust the cultivation of her mind to a circulating library".

Polly Honeycombe was Colman's first play and one of his most successful. His authorship was at first kept secret out of respect for his uncle, Lord Bath, who wanted him to make his career in the legal profession. Some people thought Garrick had written the play. In some lines which he added to Colman's prologue, he disclaimed responsibility:

> 'Tis the first folly of a simple youth,
> Caught and deluded by our harlot plays.
>
> (Printed with the play, 1760)

28

SONG IN *THE WAY TO KEEP HIM* (1761)

sung by Mrs. Cibber in the character of Widow Bellmour

Ye fair married dames, who so often deplore
That a lover once blest is a lover no more,
Attend to my counsel, nor blush to be taught
That prudence must cherish what beauty has caught.

The bloom of your cheek and the glance of your eye,   5
Your roses and lilies may make the men sigh;
But roses and lilies and sighs pass away,
And passion will die as your beauties decay.

Use the man that you wed like your fav'rite guitar.
Though music in both, they are both apt to jar;   10
How tuneful and soft from a delicate touch,
Not handled too roughly nor played on too much!

The sparrow and linnet will feed from you hand,
Grow tame by your kindness and come at command.
Exert with your husband the same happy skill,   15
For hearts, like your birds, may be tamed to your will.

Be gay and good-humoured, complying and kind;
Turn the chief of your care from your face to your mind;
'Tis there that a wife may her conquests improve,
And Hymen shall rivet the fetters of Love.   20

The text follows that published with the 4th ed. of the play, 1761 — the earliest ed. to print Garrick's song.

After being successfully performed as an afterpiece to *The Desert Island* (see 26), Arthur Murphy's *The Way to Keep Him* was enlarged from three to five acts, and the new version had its première at Drury Lane on January 10th 1761, as the mainpiece of the evening. Garrick's song was written for this enlarged version of the play. It appears to be a substitute for a song by

Murphy, which, however, retains its place in all editions of the enlarged play, where Garrick's song is printed as an appendix. The music for Garrick's song was written by Thomas Arne.

Garrick's song sums up, rather more clearly and effectively than Murphy's, the advice given by the Widow Bellmour to Mrs. Lovemore, on how to win back the affection of her husband. In the play the author of the song is Lord Etheridge, a disguise which Mr. Lovemore uses in wooing the Widow Bellmour. The part of Lovemore was played by Garrick.

29

PROLOGUE TO *EDGAR AND EMMELINE* (1761)

spoken by Mrs. Yates

Old times, old fashions and the fairies gone,
Let us return, good folks, to sixty-one,
To this blest time, ye fair, of female glory,
When pleasures unforbidden lie before ye.
No sprites to fright you now, no guardian elves.   5
Your wise directors are your own dear selves.
And every fair one feels from old to young,
While these your guides, you never can do wrong.
Weak were the sex of yore, their pleasures few.
How much more wise, more spirited are you.   10
Would any Lady Jane or Lady Mary,
Ere they did this or that, consult a fairy?
Would they permit this saucy pigmy crew
For each small slip to pinch 'em black and blue?
Well may you shudder, for with all your charms,   15
Were this the case, good heaven, what necks and arms!

Thus did they serve our grandames heretofore.
The very thought must make us moderns sore.
Did their poor hearts for cards or dancing beat,
These elves raised blisters on their hands and feet.   20
Though loo the game and fiddles played most sweetly,
They could not squeeze dear Pam nor foot Moll Peatly.
Were wives with husbands but a little wilful,
Were they at that same loo a little skilful;
Did they with pretty fellows laugh or sport,   25
Wear ruffs too small, or petticoats too short;
Did they, no matter how, disturb their clothes,
Or, over-lilied, add a little rose —
These spiteful fairies rattled round their beds
And put strange frightful nonsense in their heads.   30
Nay, while the husband snored and prudish aunt,

Had the fond wife but met the dear gallant,
Though locked the door and all as still as night,
Pop through the keyhole whips the fairy sprite,
Trips round the room — "My husband!" madam cries —   35
"The devil! Where?" the frighted beau replies —
Jumps through the window — she calls out in vain.
He, cured of love and cooled with drenching rain,
Swears — dem him if he'll e'er intrigue again!
These were their tricks of old. But, all allow,   40
No childish fears disturb our fair ones now.

Ladies, for all this trifling, 'twould be best
To keep a little fairy in your breast;
Not one that should with moderate passions war,
But just to tweak you when you go too far.   45

The text follows that published with the play, 1761.

Edgar and Emmeline. A Fairy Tale, by Dr. John Hawkesworth, was first performed at Drury Lane on January 31st 1761. Garrick's epilogue enlarges wittily upon the function which fairies have in the play, where they act as guardians of human beings. For both Edgar, son of the Earl of Kent, and Emmeline, daughter of the Earl of Northumberland, it has been ordained that they will not find happiness in marriage unless their first relationship with the one they are to marry is one of friendship and mutual esteem, rather than sexual love. To bring this situation about, the fairies persuade Edgar to dress up as a woman and Emmeline to dress up as a man. When they meet, both think the other is of the same sex as themselves and a friendship develops, which turns to love when the true situation is revealed to them. Mrs. Yates, the speaker of the epilogue, played the part of Emmeline.

30

MR. GARRICK'S ANSWER TO A NOBLEMAN, WHO ASKED HIM IF HE DID NOT INTEND BEING IN PARLIAMENT
(1761)

More than content with what my labours gain,
Of public favour though a little vain,
Yet not so vain my mind, so madly bent,
To wish to play the fool in Parliament;
In each dramatic unity to err,   5
Mistaking time and place and character.
Were it my fate to quit the mimic art,
I'd strut and fret no more in any part;
No more in public scenes would I engage,
Or wear the cap and mask on any stage.   10

The text printed here is found in LC *(Mar. 26-28, 1761 and Oct. 6-8, 1774),* BC *(April 2, 1761),* LM *(April 1761),* AR *(1761),* Yearly Chronicle *(1762),* LEP *(Oct. 4-6, 1774),* MC *(Oct. 7, 1774),* UM *(Oct. 1776),* NFHW *and* Kearsley, *and in two Folger transcripts and a Bodleian transcript. A Folger autograph (from which the present title is taken), an Osborn transcript, and other printed versions depart from this text only in minor details. Folger, however, has another autograph, and another transcript verbally identical with it. These give a quite different version of the poem. The autograph is dated 1752 and reads as follows:*

> To Sr George Littleton upon his asking Me If I did not intend to get into Parliament.
> Indeed Sr George, 'twas never my Intent,
> To wear y^e *Cap & Mask* in Parliament;
> To change ye Scene, & foolishly transfer,
> *My Skill,* from *Drury Lane* to *Westminster:*
> Had I my wish, I'd quit ye Mimic Art,
> Nor *Strut or fret my hour,* in any Part;
> No More in Public Life, would I Engage,
> Or Play y^e *Fool* or *Knave* on any Stage!

Presumably Garrick was not satisfied with this 1752 version of the epigram, or thought it unsuitable for publication (perhaps because of the wish expressed in it that he were in a position to leave the stage), and revised it several years later, only then allowing it to be published. (See J.D. Hainsworth, "The Date of David Garrick's Lines to George Lyttelton", Review of English Studies, *XXIV (1973), 458-60.)*

Lord Lyttelton, to whom these lines are addressed, was Sir George

Lyttelton and a prominent member of the House of Commons in 1752, when the first version of the epigram appears to have been written. He took his seat in the House of Lords in 1756. The epigram was not published until 1761. Lyttelton was himself fond of writing verse, and is included in the collection of *The English Poets* for which Johnson wrote his *Lives*.

31

EPILOGUE TO *ALL IN THE WRONG* (1761)

spoken by Mrs. Yates

Bless me, this summer work is so fatiguing!
And then our play's so bustling, so intriguing!
Such miffing, sighing, scolding, all together!
These love affairs suit best with colder weather.
At this warm time these writers should not treat you   5
With so much love and passion, for they'll heat you.
Poets, like weavers, should, with taste and reason,
Adapt their various goods to every season.
For the hot months the fanciful and slight;
For mind and body something cool and light.   10
Authors themselves, indeed, neglect this rule,
Dress warm in summer and at Christmas cool.
I told our bard within these five-act plays
Are rich brocades unfit for sultry days.
Were you a cook, said I, would you prepare   15
Large hams and roasted sirloins for your fare?
Their very smoke would pall a city glutton.
A tragedy would make you all unbutton.
Both appetites now ask for daintier picking —
Farce, pantomime, cold lamb or white-legged chicken.   20
At Ranelagh fine rolls and butter see,
Signor Tenducci and the best green tea.
Italian singing is as light as feather —
Beard is too loud, too powerful for this weather.
Vauxhall more solidly regales your palates —   25
Champagne, cantatas, cold boiled beef and ballads.
What shall we do your different tastes to hit?
You relish satire *(To the pit)*; you ragouts of wit. *(Boxes)*
Your taste is humour and high-seasoned joke; *(First gallery)*
You call for hornpipes and for "Hearts of oak".   30
                    (Second gallery)

O could I wish and have! A conjuring man
Once told my fortune and he charmed this fan—
Said with a flirt I might my will enjoy.
Think you there's magic in this little toy?
I'll try its power; and, if I gain my wish,   35
I'll give you, sirs, a downright English dish.
Come then, a song. *(Flirts and music is heard)* Indeed, I see 'twill do.
Take heed, gallants, I'll play the deuce with you.
Whene'er I please I'll charm you to my sight,
And tear a fan with flirting every night.   40

Enter two ballad singers, who sing the following song.

Ye critics above and ye critics below,
Ye finer-spun critics who keep the mid row,
O tarry a moment, I'll sing you a song
Shall prove that, like us, you are all in the wrong.

Ye poets who mount on the famed winged steed,   45
Of prancing and wincing and kicking take heed;
For when by those hornets, the critics, you're stung,
You're thrown in the dirt and are all in the wrong.

Ye actors who act what these writers have writ,
Pray stick to you poet and spare your own wit;   50
For when with your own you unbridle your tongue,
I'll hold ten to one you are all in the wrong.

Ye knaves who make news for the foolish to read,
Who print daily slanders the hungry to feed;
For a while you mislead 'em, the news-hunting throng,   55
Till the pillory proves you are all in the wrong.

Ye grave politicians, so deep and so wise,
With your hums and your shrugs and your uplifted eyes,
The road that you travel is tedious and long,
But I pray you jog on — you are all in the wrong.   60

Ye happy fond husbands and fond happy wives,
Let never suspicion embitter your lives,
Let your prudence be stout and your faith be as strong —
Who watch or who catch, they are all in the wrong.

Ye unmarried folks, be not bought or be sold,   65
Let age avoid youth and the young ones the old;

For they'll soon get together, the young with the young,
And then, my wise old ones, you're all in the wrong.

Ye soldiers and sailors who bravely have fought,
Who honour and glory and laurels have bought,   70
Let your foes but appear you'll be at 'em ding dong,
And if they come near you, they're all in the wrong.

Ye judges of taste to our labours be kind,
Our errors are many, pray wink or be blind;
Still find your way hither to glad us each night,   75
And our note we will change to: "You're all in the right."

The texts of both epilogue and song are taken from The Works of Arthur Murphy *(1786).*
Earlier printings of the play do not include either epilogue or song. The texts of epilogue
and song found in Murphy's Works *are preferred to versions printed in journals, etc.*
because they incorporate corrections in Garrick's hand in Folger transcripts. Other
printed versions of the song include a refrain at the end of each stanza. For the first eight
stanzas this reads:

> Sing tantara rara, wrong all, wrong all,
> Sing tantara rara, all wrong.

For the ninth stanza this is changed to:

> Sing tantara rara, right all, right all,
> Sing tantara rara, all right.

The refrain is crossed out in the Folger transcript of the song corrected by Garrick.

The stage direction in line 37 is taken from GM *(June 1761). Murphy's* Works *reads*
(Music is heard).

For an alternative ending to the epilogue, to be used if Murphy wishes to dispense with
the song, see Letters, *No. 269.*

Samuel Foote and Arthur Murphy were partners in renting Drury Lane
for the summer of 1761. *All in the Wrong*, a new comedy by Murphy, opened
the season on June 15th. It was based on Molière's *Sganarelle, ou le cocu*
imaginaire.

Mrs. Yates's graceful deployment of her fan throughout the epilogue
must have added considerably to the audience's pleasure. In the comedy, she
had played the part of Belinda, a young lady with a foolishly jealous lover.
Belinda herself comes to believe, quite wrongly, that her lover is unfaithful.
Mrs. Yates's husband, Richard Yates, had played the role of Sir John Restless,
a husband with foolish suspicions about his wife. He was one of the singers of
the song following the epilogue. According to a transcript in the Harvard
Theatre Collection, Mr. Somers was the other singer.

32

THE FRIBBLERIAD (1761)

Who is this scribbler, XYZ,
Who still writes on, though little read,
Whose falsehood, malice, envy, spite,
So often grin, yet seldom bite?
Say, Garrick, does he write for bread,   5
This friend of yours, this XYZ?
For pleasure sure, not bread — 'twere vain
To write for that he ne'er could gain:
No calls of nature to excuse him,
He deals in rancour to amuse him.   10
A man it seems — 'tis hard to say.
A woman then? A moment, pray —
Unknown as yet by sex or feature,
Suppose we try to guess the creature,
Whether a wit or a pretender,   15
Of masculine or female gender.

Some things it does may pass for either,
And some it does belong to neither.
It is so fibbing, slandering, spiteful,
In phrase so dainty, so delightful,   20
So fond of all it reads and writes,
So waggish when the maggot bites:
Such spleen, such wickedness and whim,
It must be woman and a brim.
But then the learning and the Latin!   25
The ends of Horace come so pat in,
And wanting wit, it makes such shift
To fill up gaps with Pope and Swift,
As cunning housewives bait their traps,
And take their game with bits and scraps;   30
For playhouse critics, keen as mice,
Are ever greedy, never nice;
And rank abuse, like toasted cheese,

Will catch as many as you please.
In short, 'tis easily discerning,   35
By here and there a patch of learning,
The creature's male — say all we can,
It must be something like a man.
What, like a man from day to shrink,
And seek revenge with pen and ink?   40
On mischief bent his name conceal,
And like a toad in secret steal;
There swell with venom inward pent
Till out he crawls to give it vent.
Hate joined with fear will shun the light,   45
But hate and manhood fairly fight —
'Tis manhood's mark to face the foe,
And not in ambush give the blow.
The savage thus, less man than beast,
Upon his foe will fall and feast,   50
From bush or hole his arrows send,
To wound his prey, then tear and rend;
For fear and hatred in conjunction,
Make wretches that feel no compunction.

With colours flying, beat of drum,   55
Unlike to this see Churchill come.
And now like Hercules he stands,
Unmasked his face but armed his hands;
Alike prepared to write or drub,
This holds a pen, and that a club —   60
A club which nerves like his can wield,
And formed a wit like his to shield.
Mine is the *Rosciad*, mine, he cries;
Who says 'tis not I say he lies.
To falsehood and to fear a stranger,   65
Not one shall share my fame or danger.
Let those who write with fear or shame,
Those *Craftsmen* scribblers, hide their name.
My name is Churchill. Thus he spoke
And thrice he waved his knotted oak.   70
That done, he paused, prepared the blow,
Impartial bard, for friend and foe.

64

If such are manhood's feats and plan,
Poor XYZ will prove no man.
Nor male, nor female? Then, on oath,   75
We safely may pronounce it both.

What, of that wriggling, fribbling race,
The curse of nature and disgrace?
That mixture base, which fiends sent forth
To taint and vilify all worth;   80
Whose rancour knows nor bounds nor measure,
Feels every passion, tastes no pleasure;
The want of power all peace destroying,
For ever wishing, ne'er enjoying —
So smiling, smirking, soft in feature,   85
You'd swear it was the gentlest creature —
But touch its pride, the lady-fellow,
From sickly pale turns deadly yellow —
Male, female, vanish, fiends appear,
And all is malice, rage and fear.   90
What in the heart breeds all this evil,
Makes man on earth a very devil,
Corrupts the mind and tortures sense?
Malignity with impotence.

Say Gossip Muse, who lov'st to prattle   95
And fill the town with tittle-tattle —
To tell a secret such a bliss is —
Say for what cause these master-misses
To Garrick such a hatred bore
That long they wished to pinch him sore,   100
To bind the monster hand and foot
Like Gulliver in Lilliput,
With birchen twigs to flea his skin
And each to stick him with a pin?
Are things so delicate so fell?   105
Can cherubim be imps of hell?
Tell us how spite a scheme begot,
Who laid the eggs, who hatched the plot.
O sing in namby-pamby feet,
Like to the subject tripping neat.   110
Snatch every grace that fancy reaches;
Relate their passions, plottings, speeches.

You, when their Panfribblerium sat,
Saw 'em convened and heard their chat,
Saw all their wriggling, fuming, fretting,   115
Their nodding, frisking and curvetting;
Each minute saw their rage grow stronger
Till the dear things could hold no longer,
But out burst forth the dreadful vow,
To do a deed — but when, and how,   120
And where? O Muse, thy lyre new string,
The how, the when, the where to sing!
Say in what sign the sun had entered
When these sweet souls on plotting ventured.
'Twas when the balmy breath of May   125
Makes tender lambkins sport and play,
When tenderer fribbles walk, and dare
To gather nosegays in the air;
'Twas at that time of all the year
When flowers and butterflies appear,   130
When brooding warmth on nature lies,
And circulates the blood of flies;
Then fribbles were with fribbles leaguing,
And met for plotting and intriguing.

There is a place upon a hill,   135
Where cits of pleasure take their fill,
Where hautboys scream and fiddles squeak,
To sweat the ditto once a week;
Where joy of late, unmixed with noise
Of romping girls and drunken boys —   140
Where Decency, sweet maid, appeared,
And in her hand brought Johnny Beard.
'Twas here, for public rooms are free,
They met to plot and drink their tea.
Each on a satin stool was seated,   145
Which, nicely quilted, curtained, pleated,
Did all their various skill display:
Each worked his own to grace the day.
Above the rest and set apart,
A chair was placed, where curious art   150
With lace and fringe to honour meant
Him they should choose their President.

No longer now the kettle simmers,
The smoke ascends, or cotton glimmers;
The tea was done, the cups reversed.   155
Lord Trip began — "May I be cursed:
May this right hand grow brown and speckled,
This nose be pimpled, face be freckled,
May my sick monkey ne'er get up,
May my sweet Dido die in pup,   160
Nay, may I meet a worse disaster,
My finger cut and have no plaster,
No cordial drops when dead with vapour,
Be taken short and have no paper,
If I don't feel your wrongs and shame   165
With such a zeal for fribble fame —
So much my heart for vengeance thumps,
You see it raging through my jumps."
Then opening wide his milk-white vest,
They saw it fluttering in its nest.   170
Some felt his heart, and some propose
Their drops, his lordship to compose.
The perturbation, all agree,
Was partly fidgets, partly tea.
While some the drops, some water get,   175
Sir Cock-a-doodle, baronet,
Arose — "Let not this accident
The business of the day prevent.
That Lord 's my friend, my near relation,
But what's one lord to all our nation?   180
Friendship, to patriot eyes, looks small,
And Cock-a-doodle feels for all.
Shall one, though great, engross your care,
While still unhonoured stands that chair?
Might I presume to name a creter   185
Formed for the place by art and nater,
I would a dainty wit propose
To serve our friends, destroy our foes;
To fill the chair so nicely fit,
His pride and passion match his wit.   190
Has wit has so much power and might,
It yields to nothing but his spite —

For wit may have its ebbs and flows,
But malice no abatement knows."
"Propose!" they cried, "we trust in you —   195
Name him, Sir Cock-a-doodle — do."
"Would you have one can joke and scribble,
Whose heart and very soul is fribble?
Would you have one can smile, be civil,
Yet all within a very devil —   200
Lay pretty schemes, like cobwebs spin 'em,
To catch your hated foe within 'em?
Let him a thousand times break through 'em,
The ingenious creter shall renew 'em.
If mischief is your wish and plan,   205
Let Fizgig*, Fizgig, be the man.
What say, brethren, shall it be?
Has he your voice?" All cried *"Oui, oui."*
At which one larger than the rest,
With visage sleek and swelling chest,   210
With stretched-out fingers and a thumb
Stuck to his hips, and jutting bum,
Rose up — all knew his smirking air —
They clapped and cried "The chair, the chair!"
He smiled and to the honoured seat   215
Paddled away with mincing feet.
So have I seen on dove-house top,
With cocked-up tail and swelling crop,
A pouting pigeon waddling run,
Shuffling, wriggling, noddling on.   220

Some minutes passed in forms and greeting —
Phil Whiffle oped the cause of meeting.

"In forty-eight, I well remember —
Twelve years or more, the month November —
May we no more such misery know —   225
Since Garrick made our sex a show,
And gave us up to such rude laughter
That few, 'twas said, could hold their water.
For he, that player, so mocked our motions,

---

* Some say Fitzgig. The reader may take his choice. (Garrick's footnote)

68

Our dress, amusements, fancies, notions,   230
So lisped our words and minced our steps,
He made us pass for demi-reps.
Though wisely then we laughed it off,
We'll now return his wicked scoff.
Genteel revenge is ever slow,   235
The dear Italians poison so.
But how attack him — far or near?
In front, my friends, or in the rear?"
All started up at once to speak,
As if they felt some sudden tweak.   240
'Twas quick resentment caused the smart,
And pierced them in the tenderest part.
For these dear souls are like a spinnet,
Which has both sharp and sweet within it:
Press but the keys, up start the quills;   245
And thus perked up these Jack-my-Gills.
Each touching, brushing as they rose,
Together rustled all their clothes.
Thus when, all hushed, at Handel's air,
Sit, book in hand, the British fair,   250
A sudden whiz the ear receives,
When rustling, bustling, turn the leaves.

In all the dignity of form
The chairman rose to hush the storm,
To order called, and tried to frown —   225
As all got up, so all sat down.
Sir Diddle then he thus addressed:
" 'Tis yours to speak; be mute the rest."
When thus the knight: "Can I dissemble,
Conceal my rage while thus I tremble?   260
O Fizgig, 'tis that Garrick's name
Now stops my voice and shakes my frame!
His pangs would please, his death — oh lud! —
Blood, Mr. Fizgig, blood, blood, blood!"
The thought, too mighty for his mind,   265
O'ercame his powers — he stared — grew blind —
Cold sweat his faded cheek o'erspread,
Like dew upon the lily's head.
He squeaked and sighed, no more could say

But "Blood, bloo-, blo-," and died away. 270
Thus when in war a hero swoons,
With loss of blood or fear of wounds,
They bear him off — and thus they bore
Sir Diddle to the garden door,
Where sat Lord Trip, where stood for use 275
Salts, hartshorn, peppermint and eau-de-luce.

A pause ensued, at length began
The valiant captain, Pattypan.
With kimboed arm and tossing head
He bridled up — "Wear I this red? 280
Shall blood be named and I be dumb?
For that and that alone I come.
Glory's my call and blood my trade,
And thus" — then forth he drew his blade.
At once the whole assembly shrieks, 285
At once the roses quit their cheeks;
Each face o'ercast with deadly white,
Not paint itself could stand the fright.
The roof with "Order, order!" rings,
And all cry out "No naked things!" 290
The captain sheathed his wrath and pride
And stuck the bodkin by his side.

More soft, more gentle than a lamb,
The Reverend Mister Marjoram
Arose — but first with finger's tip 295
He pats the patch upon his lip,
Then o'er it glides his healing tongue,
And thus he said — or, rather, sung:
"Sure, 'tis the error of the moon.
What, fight a mimic, a buffoon? 300
In France he has the church's curse,
And England's church is ten times worse.
Have you not read the holy writ
Just published by a reverend wit,
That every actor is a thing, 305
A merry-andrew, paper king,
A puppet made of rags and wood,
The lowest son of earth, mere mud;

Mere public game, where'er you meet him,
And cobblers as they please may treat him;   310
Slave, coxcomb, venal, and what not,
Ten thousand names that I've forgot?
Then risk not thus a precious life
In such a low, unnat'rel strife,
And sure, to stab him would be cruel —   315
I vote for arsenic in his gruel."

He said and smiled, then sunk with grace,
Licked the patched lip and wiped his face.
A buzz of rapture filled the room,
Like bees about a shrub in bloom.   320
All whispered round: "Was it not fine?"
"O very — very — 'twas divine!"
But soon as from the chair was seen
A waving hand and speaking mein,
A calm came on. The chairman bowed   325
And, smirking, spoke: "I'm pleased and proud
To mix my sentiments with yours —
'Tis prudence every point secures.
Two friends with rapture I have heard —
One favours arsenic, one the sword.   330
In both there's danger, but, succeeding,
Short pangs in poisoning, less in bleeding.
A sudden death 's not worth a shilling —
I'd have our foe nine years a-killing."
Then from his bosom forth he drew   335
A crow-quill pen — "Behold for you
And your revenge, this instrument.
From hell it came, to me 'twas sent.
Within is poison, sword and all,
Its point a dagger, dipped in gall.   340
Keen, lingering pangs the foe shall feel,
While clouds the hand that stabs conceal.
With this, while living, I'll dissect him,
Create his errors, then detect 'em;
Swell tiny faults to monstrous size,   345
Then point 'em out to purblind eyes;
Which, like Polonius, gaze in air

71

For ousel, camel, whale or bear.
His very merit I'll pervert,
And swear the ore is sand and dirt.   350
I know his quick and warm sensations,
And thence will work him more vexations.
Attended with some noisy cit,
Of strong belief but puny wit,
I'll take my seat, be rude and loud,   355
That each remark may reach the crowd.
At Lear we'll laugh, be hard as rocks,
And sit at Scrub like barbers' blocks.
When all is still we'll roar like thunder,
When all applause, be mute and wonder.   360
In this I boast uncommon merit —
I like, have praised, his genius, spirit;
His various powers, I own, divert me —
'Tis his success alone has hurt me.
My patriot hand like Brutus strikes,   365
And stabs and wounds where most it likes.
He, as a Roman, gave the blow;
I, as a fribble, stab your foe.
He mourned the deed, would not prevent it;
I'll do the deed, and then lament it.*"   370
At this all tongues their hearts obey,
A burst of rapture forced its way —
Bravo! Bravissimo! Huzza!

All rose at once, then, hand in hand,
Each linked to each, the heroes stand,   375
Like fairies form a magic round,
Then vow — and tremble at the sound —
By all that's dear to human kind,
By every tie can fribbles bind,
They vow that with their latest breath   380
They'll stand by Fizgig, life or death.
The kiss goes round the parting friends,
The chair is left, the assembly ends.

* Some MSS read *repent it*. (Garrick's footnote)

72

Then each, his spirits to recruit,
For biscuits called and candied fruit, 385
And sipped, his fluttered nerves to heal,
Warm water, sack, and orange-peel.
Then, made as warm as warmth could make 'em,
All to their several homes betake 'em,
Save one, who, harrassed with the chair, 390
Remained at Hampstead for the air.

Now, Garrick, for the future know
Where most you have deserved a foe.
Can you their rage with justice blame?
To you they owe their public shame. 395
Though long they slept, they were not dead;
Their malice wakes in XYZ.
And now bursts forth their treasured gall
Through him, Cock Fribble of them all.

The text follows that printed for J. Coote, 1761.

The Fribbleriad was published in 1761. An Irishman by the name of
Thomas (or Thady) Fitzpatrick, who, for reasons unknown, had grown
hostile towards Garrick, had published a series of letters attacking him in *The
Craftsman*. XYZ, the pseudonym to which Garrick refers at the beginning of
his poem, was one of those used by Fitzpatrick in these letters. The series was
subsequently republished as a pamphlet entitled *An Enquiry into the Real
Merit of a Certain Popular Performer* (1760). In his criticisms of Garrick,
Fitzpatrick goes so far as to assert that "he never did, nor ever could, speak
ten successive lines of Shakespeare with grammatical propriety" *(An Enquiry
. . ., p.23)*. Garrick knew well enough who his attacker was. *The Fribbleriad*,
in which Fizgig represents Fitzpatrick, is his reply.

A "fribler" *(sic)* had been defined by Steele in *Spectator* 288 as "one
who professes rapture and admiration for the woman to whom he addresses,
and dreads nothing so much as her consent". There is a character called
"Fribble" in Garrick's play *Miss in Her Teens*, first performed in 1747.
According to Garrick's friend, Arthur Murphy, he represents a phenomenon
of the times, "the pretty gentlemen, who chose to unsex themselves, and
make a display of delicacy that exceeded female softness" *(Life, I, 118)*. In
the course of acting the role of Fribble, Garrick was said to mimic eleven

fashionable gentlemen of the time (see *The Autobiography and Corres-pondence of Mary Granville, Mrs. Delany,* ed. Lady Llanover, London, 1861, II, 453). In *The Fribbleriad,* Garrick comically takes it for granted that Fitzpatrick's attacks on him are a belated act of vengeance, prompted by "fribbles" who recognized themselves in the play.

The Fribbleriad recalls *Miss in Her Teens* in several details. Thus the affected speech of the fribbles in the poem (e.g. "creter", line 185) is also one of the characteristics of Fribble in the play (see 5); Captain Pattypan in the poem recalls Flash in the play; and Lord Trip, Phil Whiffle and Sir Diddle, who are named as fribbles in the poem, are amongst Fribble's associates in the play.

In the "Advertisement" to his poem, Garrick draws attention to its mock-heroic qualities:

> It may properly be called an *Iliad* in a nutshell; for though it does not consist of many more than 400 lines, it contains all the essential epic properties — the plan, sentiments, character, diction, moral, metre, and even the heroes themselves, all in miniature. *(Fribbleriad,* p. vii)

Fitzpatrick's animosity towards Garrick was to find a further outlet in the Half-Price Riots of 1763. At both Drury Lane and Covent Garden, the concession by which theatregoers were allowed in for half-price after the third act, was suspended when a new play was being performed. Fitzpatrick objected to this policy, and stirred up riots at Drury Lane on January 25th and 26th 1763, and later at Covent Garden. During the first riot substantial damage was done to the theatre. On the second evening Garrick capitulated.

Charles Churchill's poem *The Rosciad,* to which *The Fribbleriad* refers, went into its eighth edition in the year of the Half-Price Riots. Churchill's eulogy of Garrick as the Roscius of the age had at first embarrassed Garrick because it was coupled with some severe criticisms of other actors, but by 1763 they were good friends. Churchill took the opportunity afforded by the eighth edition of his poem to insert a portrait of Fitzpatrick which takes up again some of the points made in *The Fribbleriad:*

> A motley figure, of the Fribble tribe,
> Which heart can scarce conceive, or pen describe,
> Came simpering on, to ascertain whose sex
> Twelve sage impanelled matrons would perplex.
> Nor male, nor female; neither and yet both;
> Of neuter gender, though of Irish growth.

> *(Rosciad,* lines 141-46)

33

EPILOGUE TO *ELVIRA* (1763)

spoken by Mrs. Cibber

Ladies and gentlemen — 'tis so ill-bred —
We have no epilogue because I'm dead.
For he, our bard, with frenzy-rolling eye,
Swears you shan't laugh when he has made you cry.
At which I gave his sleeve a gentle pull: 5
Suppose they should not cry and should be dull.
In such a case 'twould surely do no harm,
A little lively nonsense taken warm.
On critic stomachs delicate and queasy,
'Twill even make a heavy meal sit easy.   10
"The town hates epilogues." It is not true.
I answered that for you — and you — and you.
                              (To pit, boxes, and first gallery)
They call for epilogues and hornpipes too.
                              (Looking at the upper gallery)
"Madam," the critics say — to you they're civil.
Here, if they have 'em not, they'll play the devil.   15
Out of this house, sir, and to you alone,
They'll smile, cry "Bravo!" "Charming!" Here they groan.
A single critic will not frown, look big,
Harmless and pliant as a single twig;
But crowded here they change and 'tis not odd,   20
For twigs, when bundled up, become a rod.
Critics to bards, like beauties to each other,
When tête-à-tête their enmity they smother:
"Kiss me, my dear." "How do you?" "Charming creature!"
"What shape, what bloom, what spirit in each feature!"   25
"You flatter me." " 'Pon honour, no." "You do."
"My friend!" "My dear!" "Sincerely yours." "Adieu."
But when at routs, the dear friends change their tone —
I speak of foreign ladies, not our own.
Will you permit, good sirs, these gloomy folk   30

To give all tragedy without one joke?
They gravely tell us tragedy's designed
To purge the passions, purify the mind.
To which I say, to strike those blockheads dumb,
With physic always give a sugar-plum.   35
I love these sugar-plums in prose or rhymes —
No one is merrier than myself sometimes.
Yet I, poor I, with tears and constant moan,
Am melted down almost to skin and bone.
This night in sighs and sobs I drew my breath;   40
Love, marriage, treason, prison, poison, death,
Were scarce sufficient to complete my fate —
Two children were thrown in to make up weight.
With all these sufferings, is it not provoking
To be denied at last a little joking?   45
If they will make new laws, for mirth's sake break 'em.
Roar out for epilogues and let me speak 'em.

The text follows that published with the play, 1763.

David Mallet's tragedy, *Elvira*, was first performed at Drury Lane on January 19th 1763.

The account given in the epilogue (lines 40-43) of the sufferings of Elvira (played by Mrs. Cibber) does not exaggerate. The King of Portugal insists that his son, Don Pedro, must marry Almeyda. But Don Pedro is already secretly married to Elvira, maid of honour to the Queen, and they have two children. Elvira is placed in the custody of the Queen and eventually poisoned by her. Don Pedro takes up arms against his father and is condemned to death, but finally pardoned.

Mallet, a freethinker and a supporter of the unpopular Prime Minister, the Earl of Bute, had many enemies. Amongst these was James Boswell, who tried to get *Elvira* damned at its opening performance (see Introduction, p. xx). Subsequently Boswell contributed to a pamphlet of *Critical Structures on the New Tragedy of "Elvira"*. Edward Gibbon, on the other hand, records how he went to the first performance with Mallet and about thirty of his friends "ready to silence all opposition", but they had no occasion to exert themselves (see *Gibbon's Journal*, pp. 202-03).

The controversy, referred to in the epilogue, as to whether or not it was proper for a tragedy to be followed by a comic epilogue, had been going on for a long time. Allardyce Nicoll *(A History of Early Eighteenth Century Drama, 1700-1750*, London, 1925, pp. 64-66) cites numerous epilogues which touch on this, the earliest of them being that to William Phillips's *Belisarius* (1724). A still earlier protest against the practice is in a letter by "Physibulus" (presumably the work of Joseph Addison or Richard Steele or Eustace Budgell) in *Spectator* 338. The occasion for this was the publication of Ambrose Philips's tragedy *The Distressed Mother* (1712), with its comic epilogue by Budgell. This letter allowed Budgell to write a defence of his practice in *Spectator* 341. Epilogues, he argues, "are distinct performances by themselves, pieces entirely detached from the play, and no way essential to it." As for the speaker of his epilogue — Mrs. Oldfield, who had played Andromache, the tragic heroine, in the play — "The moment the play ends, Mrs. Oldfield is no more Andromache, but Mrs. Oldfield."

34

EPILOGUE TO *THE DISCOVERY (1763)*

spoken by Mrs. Pritchard

What strange old maggots fill an author's pate!
A female court of justice — rare conceit!
Ladies, I give you joy of your new stations.
I think you've had a trial — of your patience.
What, five long acts, and not one pleasant sally,   5
But grave Sir Anthony's attempt to rally —
No sprightly rendezvous, no pretty fellows,
No wife intriguing, nor no husband jealous!
If to such innovations you submit,
And swallow tame morality for wit,   10
If such dull rules you let a woman teach,
Her next attempt, perhaps, will be to preach.
I told her, for it vexed me to the heart —
Madam, excuse me, I don't like my part;
'Tis out of nature, never drawn from life.   15
Who ever heard of such a passive wife?
To bear so much — 'tis not in flesh and blood —
Such females might have lived before the flood.
But now the character will seem so flat —
Give *me* threats, tears, hysterics and all that —   20
If this don't work upon my lord, I hope
You'll so contrive the plot I may elope.
Take my advice, I think I know the town,
Without such aids your piece will scarce go down.
Hold, friend, she cried — I think I've hit the way   25
To reconcile both sexes to the play;
For, while the prologue bids our own be sovereign,
The scenes instruct the other how to govern.
A harmless plot — with credit to dismiss
The piece — you know the ladies never hiss.   30
And though they should condemn it, yet the men sure

Will leave a woman's faults to women's censure.
They, prone to meekness, charity and love,
Are always silent where they can't approve.
But if at loud applause we dare to aim,   35
It is the men must ratify our claim.

*The text follows that published with the 2nd ed. of the play, 1763, in which an error in
the text published with the 1st ed. is corrected. The version printed in SJC (Feb. 3-5,
1763) and several other journals differs substantially from this in its opening and
concluding lines and is the version that was submitted to the censor (Huntington,
Larpent 219).*

1-4   SJC *substitutes:*
        Well, ladies, will you patronise or no?
        Is our piece good or bad, or is't so-so?
        Pray speak your minds — ladies — with fear we wait.
        Shall we retire? Perhaps you would debate.
        Can you determine, when for truth you're seeking,
        So great a point without a little speaking?
        Yet, ere you grant our female bard protection,
        Let me, a woman, make one strong objection.

23-36   SJC *substitutes:*
        For after so much barbarous usage, sure,
        You may indulge me with one small amour.
        But if my conduct must be tame and starch,
        Season my language, make it rich and arch.
        My friend, she cried, must I new plan the part,
        And make my pen run counter to my heart?
        Too oft has ribaldry's indecent mien,
        Tricked out by female hands, disgraced the scene.
        Let me to this one merit lay my claim,
        Not to debase my sex to raise my name.

The Discovery, a comedy by Mrs. Frances Sheridan, was first performed
at Drury Lane on February 3rd 1763.

Mrs. Pritchard, as the wife of Lord Medley in the play, had indeed, as
she complains in the epilogue, to put up with a good deal. Lord Medway
(who was played by Thomas Sheridan, the dramatist's husband and the father
of Richard Brinsley Sheridan) seeks to seduce Lady Flutter, wife of Sir Harry
Flutter, to this end encouraging this young couple in their frivolous quarrels.
Being short of money, he wants to marry his daughter, Louisa, to the elderly
Sir Anthony Branville, who will take her without a fortune, and his son to
Mrs. Knightly, a rich widow, who turns out, however, to be Lord Medway's
own daughter by a deceased Portuguese lady. Medway is brought to see the
error of his ways and all ends happily.

Garrick played Sir Anthony Branville, an old-fashioned beau, whose
affections switch from Mrs. Knightly to Louisa and back again. For the way

in which Garrick played the part, see the Introduction, p. xv.

In the prologue to the play, the dramatist had claimed the right, established by Magna Carta, to be tried by her peers — in this case, the ladies of the audience. Hence the reference to *A female court of justice* (line 2).

35

THE SICK MONKEY, A FABLE (1765)

Returned from travel to your native shore,
Again to make us laugh or cry,
To turn your back, we hope, no more,
Nor from your colours fly;

Whether you fled for health or quiet,   5
Harassed with rule or sick of riot,
Or whether you have kept us lean,
As slander says,
With lenten plays,
To make our appetites more keen;   10
Whether it be or this or that,
No matter what —
For we before the curtain see but blindly —
Now you are come
To us and home,   15
We greet you, sir, and greet you kindly.

My Muse is honest as she's bold,
A forward miss
Who loves to prate — but hold —
I quite forgot;   20
Before I tell you what she is,
I'll tell you what she's not.

No bird of prey with wild uproar,
Like Churchill, to disturb the grove;
Nor comes she, like the harmless dove,   25
To bill and coo and love,
And nothing more.

In short, to speak more plainly,
Nor be it thought I speak it vainly,
Averse to flattery and spite,   30
She is a modest, sober dame —
I wish all females were the same —
And will not scratch or bite.

She is not one of those
Who show their genius in their dress, 35
Whose inky fingers, unpinned clothes,
The slipshod shoe and snuffy nose,
Denote her wit and sluttishness;
Who with a play, like pistol cocked, in hand,
Bid managers to stand: 40

"Deliver, sir,
Your thoughts on this
Before you stir."
"But, madam — miss — "
"Your answer straight; 45
I will not wait."
" 'Tis fit you know — "
"I'll hear no reason —
This very season —
Ay or no?" 50

Not to kill more precious time,
In dropping sense to pick up rhyme,
Or, like friend Shandy, rattle,
And lose my matter in my prattle;
Without much wit digression's tame, 55
So I shall give it o'er,
And beat about the bush no more,
But start my game.

The critic's pen has various uses,
It praises now, and now abuses, 60
Does this and that
Or both together,
As fancy strikes or rhymes come pat,
Stabs with the point or tickles with the feather.

Authors, like bees, buzz round and round 65
Dramatic ground,
For all they meet
Have sharp and sweet;
They do no ill,
Would fools sit still — 70
Provoke 'em and they're dangerous things;
And every player

Should equally beware
Their honey as their stings.

Garrick, thou mighty chief of kings and queens,   75
Despotic tyrant of the scenes,
Think'st thou all human race to mock
In buskin and in sock,
And will not fools
Thy mock'ry ridicules,   80
From Chalkstone's Lord to dainty Fribble,
Rave, chatter, write,
In various ways display their spite?
For all can talk, and some can scribble.

Others again   85
Take up the pen,
In panegyric's gaudy colours paint thee;
As humour flows,
Now friends, now foes,
In prose and verse and verse and prose,   90
Bedevil thee and saint thee.

And can such critics tease thee?
And can such praises please thee?
O, if they can,
Alas, poor man,   95
No more deride
Thy neighbour's weakness, folly, pride,
But cure thy own
If thou art able,
While I make known   100
My friendship to thee in a fable.

An ape there was, an ape of merit,
A lively, sportive, pleasant thing,
Had so much fancy, whim, and spirit,
And made such sport   105
He got to court
And showed his tricks before the lion king.

Such honour gave him fame
And raised his name;
From far and near they came to see   110
This monkey prodigy.

Though none were more expert and quick
In tumbling backward o'er a stick;
Though none with a more lordly pride
And happy ease did e'er bestride   115
The rugged Russian bear;
Though he could skip it up and down,
And pick the pocket of a clown,
Or whip away his hat,
Or fondle with a cat,   120
The wonder of the fair;
This was not all, he had the art
Of acting still a higher part:
To each profession that he saw,
Physic, divinity or law,   125
He ludicrously shaped him —
So much possessed of all their notions,
Their humours, oddities and motions,
That not a soul escaped him.

In ridicule's enchanted glass   130
Whatever forms are shown,
We all can see another's face
But never find our own.
To flatter self we all incline,
For self we plan and labour: 135
"Pluck not, good sir, a hair of mine,
And you may scalp my neighbour."

Each laughed to see his friend the jest,
And praised the monkey highly,
Not openly but slily —   140
At court you find a thousand such —
But what was best,
Though there were none
By turns he did not fall upon,
Each thought himself the only one   145
The mimic could not touch.
Blest fools, who boast your happy lot
From ridicule secure,
Though leopard-stained, you see no spot,
Inimitably pure.   150

Whether the jackanapes was clever,
Or the court not over nice,
By various tricks he crept in favour,
And for those tricks had double price.
Thus Fortune, in a whim,   155
Resolved to turn his brain,
And filled his cup up to the brim,
The intoxicating cup of joy,
Which better heads than his destroy —
No wonder he was vain.   160

Whenever gossip Fame prates loud,
Envy, in turn, as loud will tattle,
And scribblers to her standard crowd,
Cry "Havoc!" and prepare for battle.
Malevolence, with lynx's eye,   165
The most minute defects will spy;
And even Friendship — shame upon our kind —
Is to those faults not always blind.

The looking up fatigues the sight,
And mortals when they soar,   170
Should they once reach a certain height,
All wish to have them lower;
And friends there are in this good town
Will lend a hand to help them down.

About, about my pen,   175
Nor lose the fable in thy railing,
But to our monkey back again,
Who found that brutes as well as men,
Have this same cursed failing.

The moment he got fame and wealth   180
(How ill exchanged for ease and health!)
The envious crew
Poor Pug pursue,
Abuse his active, pliant spirit;
But chiefly those   185
Were marked his foes,
Who felt a satire in his merit.

The dull and sluggish were the first
To show their teeth, if not to bite;

The hog, the bear, the ass had burst,   190
Had they not grunted, roared, and brayed their spite.
This furious stir
Awaked the critic cur —
Hound, greyhound, mastiff, answer to the call,
The little dogs and all.   195
The game's in view:
For man and beast
Scandal's a feast,
Where both with appetite fall to.

The bloated toad in silence stole   200
To gather poison in her hole.
As mischief never knows delay,
She roused the viper in her way,
A neighbour, and her bosom friend;
For though she crawled and could not run,   205
She kept this maxim strictly
(Ye sons of Law, attend!)
That mischief, if it must be done,
'Twere well it were done quickly.

But then his friends — did they oppose?   210
(A luke-warm friend's the worst of foes.)
The goat looked wise and wagged his beard;
The spaniel shook his ears;
The fox turned up his pointed nose;
Thoughtful and dull the cat appeared,   215
Or else in whispers purred her fears;
The steed alone was firm and fast,
The generous steed stood by him to the last.

Pug sickens, mopes, and looks like death,
Speaks faintly and scarce draws his breath;   220
Some call it megrim, some the spleen —
Words often used that little mean;
But Scandal, with her face demure,
Hints it is heat of blood,
By which is understood   225
An old amour:
In short, they ransack all diseases,
And give him that their fancy pleases.
Among the rest,

That fits him best 230
Which best the doctor serves,
Of which he most avails him
When knowledge fails him,
And, with a face of wisdom, calls it — nerves.

The horse, who saw his friend's distress, 235
Did thus his honest mind express:
"Come, prithee rouse; this life's the devil.
What, sigh and sob and keep within?
What you, who used to frisk and revel,
For ever chatter and for ever grin? 240
Zounds, it would make a parson swear!
Get on my back and take the air."
Away they went, and as they pass
The hog, the dog, the bear, the ass,
Pug's different foes in different places, 245
If in the least they showed their spite,
The horse would whinny, snort, and bite,
And throw the dirt into their faces.

For all this care,
This exercise and air, 250
Yet still the monkey pined;
For well we are assured
That when the grief is in the mind,
'Tis sooner got than cured.

In this condition, 255
What to prescribe him? A physician.
There is a certain way of life
Which all must take
For fashion's sake,
Or be with all the world at strife: 260
The rich must to the doctor give,
The poor to Nature trust, and live.

It must be so — or could the tribe
Of those who quack, or who prescribe,
In folly find such ample gain? 265
Could nostrums swell the *Advertiser*,
Or the wise heads of Warwick Lane
Buy wig enough to make them wiser?

Our patient cannot wait.
"Send for a doctor straight." 270
But not a formal, half-bred fool,
Who cures by chance and kills by rule,
A periwig-pated block.
Physicians for the brutes were fowls,
And though the sworn practitioners were owls, 275
They chose a neighbouring cock.

He enters with a stately tread,
His comb and wattles dignify his head:
No outward sign was ever seen 280
That promised half so much within;
And yet (ye sons of Physic, blush!)
The wine was better than the bush.
His learning, backed by penetration,
A kind of Radcliffe-inspiration,
Bound by no partial, pedant laws, 285
Shot through each symptom to its cause —
A rarity without dispute.
He was an honest cock to boot.
Yet with this genius, worth and knowledge,
He had a stain, a deep disgrace 290
No mortal merit could efface —
He was not of the College.

But hold — our hero out of sight,
Must now again be brought to light.
We left him in the doctor's care, 295
Who with a serious face
Attending to the case,
Did thus his mind declare:

"I could, like any learned brother,
With a hard name my ignorance smother. 300
'Tis one of our established laws,
Which daily we fulfil,
Whene'er our skill can't find a cause,
To make a cause to suit our skill.
Thus we seldom meet disgrace; 305
We only can mistake the case.
What are these papers by your side?"
" 'Tis physic, sir, to cure my pride:

This heap of papers, verse and prose,
Is the joint malice of my foes;   310
There's not a day but something's sent me,
To fret me and torment me."

This said, the conversation stops,
For Pug was faint and calls for drops.
With rage subdued, the patient panted,   315
Which struck a light the doctor wanted,
Who thus pronounced: "I know your ail;
'Tis not in your heart or head,
As some have said."
"Where then, good Doctor?" "In your tail."   320

His tail of most uncommon make,
In action like the serpent kind,
A thousand different forms could take,
Twirl, twist and vary to his mind.
If lords were aped, this pliant queue   325
Was cross his breast a ribbon blue,
Or green, or red; and then, slap-dash,
A chaplain's scarf or colonel's sash.
Whene'er the city struck his brain,
'Twas round his neck a lord mayor's chain;   330
Or were his part to lisp and trip it,
Hey presto, 'twas a lady's tippet!
But now deprived of spirit, life, and strength,
It lies a languid, lank, inanimated length.

The Doctor paused, then silence broke: 335
"I'll strike a master stroke.
This tail of yours we must amend,
Give it new life and force,
And if we gain that end,
The rest will come of course.   340
With that same malice of your foes,
Both verse and prose,
Curl it each night and morning;
But then take warning
Never again to cast your eyes   345
On what is wrote, or may be writ,
Whether it is or is not wit —
For there the magic lies."

'Tis best by craft and not by book,
To cure these mental fevers. 350
The monkey all for gospel took —
The sick are great believers.
So well the doctor's words he noted,
His tail that night was papilloted;
His greedy eyes, to cure his head, 355
No more on paper-diet fed.

The cause removed, effects will cease:
Deprived of oil the flame goes out.
Our ape began to be at peace,
His tail to move about. 360
The more 'twas curled,
The more it twirled;
With head and heart
The tail took part,
Life frisks in every vein: 365
Pug was himself again.

The monkey got his health,
The doctor wealth —
Of patients he had plenty;
For though the cure was half a joke, 370
'Twas wondered at by silly folk,
And that's nineteen in twenty.
To fix his cure, historians say,
That, like Sir Wilful in the play,
He talked of foreign parts; 375
Left all his griefs and cares behind,
Sailed with the first fair wind,
And hey for Italy and arts!

What he got there no creature knows,
Nor he himself can tell us; 380
What lightly comes as lightly goes
With all such pretty fellows.
He skipped the country o'er,
And then returned
With what he learned, 385
A greater monkey than before.

The fable told, the moral comes:

Garrick, don't fret and bite your thumbs,
But take the monkey's place;
The same's your case;   390
The same prescription we advise.
Should spleen and spite —
Nay, though critic truth should write
(For who is always in the right?) —
Shut your ears and close your eyes.   395
Whate'er is published, buy the heap —
You'll have it cheap —
But not to read or hear it read:
Would you strike detraction dead,
The doctor's method cannot fail;   400
Keep the poison from your head,
And clap it to your tail.

The text follows that "Printed for J. Fletcher and Co.", 1765.

The fable was written in the spring of 1765, when Garrick was in France at the end of an eighteen months' continental tour. He was extremely anxious about the kind of reception he would get on his return home. His anxiety can be explained on various counts. The season before his departure from London had seen the Half-Price Riots at Drury Lane (see commentary on 32). That had been a season, too, in which his popularity as an actor had noticeably declined, and the public had preferred to go to see the operas which John Beard, the new manager at Covent Garden, was putting on. Now the news from London was that the crowds had returned to Drury Lane, attracted by a young actor, William Powell, whom Garrick had taken on just before he left. Garrick was jealous. As well as all this, he had been seriously ill while abroad, and the doctors were still warning him of the danger to his health if he exerted himself too much on the stage.

The Sick Monkey is, in the first place, a "puff" to draw attention to Garrick's homecoming. The puff is disguised by the uncomplimentary comparison of Garrick to an ape who performs fairground tricks for the delectation of the audience. The poem is also a vindication of Garrick in relation to his enemies and detractors, whom he feared might return to the attack now that he was coming back among them. It was, of course, essential to Garrick's purposes that the authorship of the poem should be concealed. His anxiety on this score is shown by his instructions to his friend, George Colman, to whom he sent the poem. The publisher, a known associate of Garrick, was to adopt a false name, the printer to be sworn to secrecy, and

Colman to burn an incriminating letter from Garrick (see *Letters*, Nos. 352, 355). In fact, the publication of *The Sick Monkey*, a few days after Garrick's arrival in London, made little impact.

In its metrical irregularity, *The Sick Monkey* appears to be influenced by Sir John Vanbrugh's play *Aesop* (1696), which was still being performed in Garrick's day. In the course of this a number of fables are told, couched in a similarly irregular metrical form.

36

QUIN'S SOLILOQUY ON SEEING DUKE HUMPHREY
AT ST. ALBANS (1765)

A plague on Egypt's arts I say.
Embalm the dead — on senseless clay
   Rich wines and spices waste!
Like sturgeon or like brawn shall I,
Bound in a precious pickle, lie,   5
   Which I can never taste?

Let me embalm this flesh of mine
With turtle fat and Bordeaux wine,
   And spoil the Egyptian trade.
Than Humphrey's Duke more happy I: 10
Embalmed *alive*, old Quin shall die
   A mummy ready-made.

The text follows that published in SJC *(Sept. 7-10, 1765),* BC *(Sept. 19, 1765),* GM *(Sept. 1765),* SM *(Sept. 1765),* The Life of James Quin, Comedian, *1766,* UM *(Sept. 1775),* NFHW *and* Kearsley. *It is verbally identical with that given in the autograph and one of the two transcripts owned by Folger.*

     The date of their first publication suggests that these verses belong to 1765. This is confirmed by the anonymous (and not always reliable) *Life of Mr. James Quin, Comedian* (1766), which says that they stemmed from Quin's last visit to the Garricks at Hampton in the summer of 1765.

     The vault containing the embalmed body of Humphrey, Duke of Gloucester (1391-1447), had been discovered at St. Albans in 1703 and the Duke's body had become a tourist attraction.

     On Quin, see also 1, 16, 38, 40.

37

PROLOGUE SPOKEN TO *MUCH ADO ABOUT NOTHING,* ACTED BY COMMAND OF HIS MAJESTY (1765)

by Mr. Garrick

With doubt, joy, apprehension, almost dumb,
To face this awful court once more I come.
Lest Benedick should suffer by my fear,
Before he enters I myself am here.
I'm told (what flattery to my heart!) that you*   5
Have wished to see me, nay have pressed it too.
Alas, 'twill prove another *Much Ado!*
I, like a boy who long has truant played,
No lessons got, no exercises made,
On bloody Monday takes his fearful stand,   10
And often eyes the birchen-sceptred hand.
'Tis twice twelve years since first the stage I trod,
Enjoyed your smiles and felt the critic's rod.
A very ninepin I, my stage-life through,
Knocked down by wits, set up again by you.   15
In four-and-twenty years the spirits cool.
Is it not long enough to play the fool?
To prove it is, permit me to repeat
What late I heard in passing through the street.
A youth of parts, with ladies by his side,   20
Thus cocked his glass and through it shot my pride.
" 'Tis he, by Jove, grown quite a clumsy fellow.
He's fit for nothing but a Punchinello."
"O yes, for comic scenes — Sir John — no further.
He's much too fat for battles, rapes and murder."   25
Worn in the service, you my faults will spare,
And make allowance for the wear and tear.

Looking at, and respectfully bowing to His Majesty.

The Chelsea pensioner, who, rich in scars,
Fights o'er in prattle all his former wars,
Though past the service, may the young ones teach   30
To march, present, to fire and mount the breach.
Should the drum beat to arms, at first he'll grieve
For wooden leg, lost eye and armless sleeve;
Then cocks his hat, looks fierce and swells his chest:
" 'Tis for my King, and, zounds, I'll do my best!"   35

The text printed here is found in SJC *(Dec. 5-7, 1765),* L1 EP *(Dec. 6-9, 1765),* BC *(Dec. 12, 1765),* GM, *(Dec. 1765),* LM *(Dec. 1765),* CT, CS *and* EE. *A number of other publications –* PA *(Dec. 9, 1765),* LC *(Dec. 7-10, 1765),* RM *(Dec. 1765),* UM *(Dec. 1765),* Universal Museum *(Dec. 1765),* OPE, ETW, SC, TB *and Kearsley – depart from this text only at lines 2, 10 and 11. A choice between these two versions of the prologue can only be quite arbitrary.*

2   PA *etc. read:*
       Once more to face this awful court I come.

10   PA *etc. read* take my *for* takes his.

11   PA *etc. read* eye *for* eyes.

The footnote relating to line 5 is from Kearsley. Elsewhere, the corresponding footnote reads The Audience. *Since the prologue was spoken on some evenings when the King was not present, as well as at the royal command performance, this discrepancy is understandable.*

This prologue was called for and spoken at another royal command performance on Dec. 5, 1765, when Garrick was playing the part of Sir John Brute in Vanbrugh's The Provoked Wife. *For his next appearance on the stage, which was on Dec. 13, in this same role, Garrick had ready some new and more appropriate opening lines. Folger has a transcript of these, and an autograph which gives what appears to be an earlier version of them. The transcript reads as follows:*

What Still this prologue, tho' the Spirits fled!
Bottled Small Beer's the Devil – when 'tis dead.
Prologues, & Epilogues were heretofore,
Heard once, or twice, or thrice, & then no more;
You for those dead & gone, will call & hiss,
When Spoke, you Stare, & ask, – what is all this?
And the poor Speaker, wretched all the while,
Must lively seem, & Grin – a ghastly Smile;
What 'tis to Smile in Grief, You cannot guess,
I saw a fidler once in this distress,
Who forc'd to play amidst his Childrens Cries,
Jigg'd with his hands, whilst tears ran down his Eyes.

When I for Sir John Brute have set my face,
You call for prologue – quickly I uncase
Must change from top to toe, – without – within –
Thro' my fixt features, force a Spurious Grin –
And tho' distrest, must Smiling thus begin

'Tis twice Twelve Years &c –

This performance of *Much Ado About Nothing*, by royal command, with Garrick as Benedick, was at Drury Lane on November 14th 1765. This was Garrick's first appearance on the stage since his return, in April 1765, from his eighteen months on the Continent. Garrick had seriously considered retirement both from acting and management — or, at least, from acting (see *Letters*, Nos. 357, 358, 368, 373). He was already possessed of a substantial fortune, and was forty-nine years old and not in the best of health. Moreover, the season before his departure abroad had not been a happy one (see commentary on 35). The royal command performance appears to have been arranged through influential friends, with, of course, Garrick's connivance (see *Letters*, No. 373 and Boaden, I, 201). The enthusiasm of a packed house helped to convince Garrick that he should continue both as actor and manager, while restricting the number of his appearances on stage.

38

PROLOGUE TO *THE CLANDESTINE MARRIAGE* (1766)

spoken by Mr. Holland

Poets and painters, who from Nature draw
Their best and richest stores, have made this law:
That each should neighbourly assist his brother,
And steal with decency from one another.
Tonight, your matchless Hogarth gives the thought,   5
Which from his canvas to the stage is brought.
And who so fit to warm the poet's mind
As he who pictured morals and mankind?
But not the same their characters and scenes;
Both labour for one end by different means.   10
Each, as it suits him, takes a separate road,
Their one great object *Marriage à la mode:*
Where titles deign with cits to have and hold,
And change rich blood for more substantial gold;
And honoured trade from interest turns aside,   15
To hazard happiness for titled pride.
The painter dead, yet still he charms the eye;
While England lives his fame can never die.
But he who struts his hour upon the stage
Can scarce extend his fame for half an age.   20
Nor pen nor pencil can the actor save,
The art and artist share one common grave.

O let me drop one tributary tear
On poor Jack Falstaff's grave and Juliet's bier.
You to their worth must testimony give;   25
'Tis in your hearts alone their fame can live.
Still as the scenes of life will shift away,
The strong impressions of their art decay.
Your children cannot feel what you have known;
They'll boast of Quins and Cibbers of their own.   30
The greatest glory of our happy few
Is to be felt and be approved by you.

The text follows that published with the play, 1766.

The *Clandestine Marriage*, a comedy by George Colman and David Garrick, was first performed at Drury Lane on February 20th 1766. Colman (1732-94) had begun his career as a dramatist with *Polly Honeycombe* (see 27). He and Garrick had become close friends but their collaboration in *The Clandestine Marriage* led to a temporary breach in this relationship. Garrick, having determined, on grounds of health, not to undertake any new stage roles, offended Colman by declining to play the part of Lord Ogleby in *The Clandestine Marriage* and petty recriminations followed.

William Hogarth, also a friend of Garrick's (see 15), to whose series of paintings, "Marriage à la Mode", Garrick acknowledges indebtedness for the portrayal of society in the play, had died in October 1764.

The Falstaff referred to in the prologue is James Quin (see 1, 16, 36, 40), one of whose finest roles this was. The Juliet referred to is Mrs. Susannah Cibber. Both had died in January 1766.

39

EPILOGUE TO *THE CLANDESTINE MARRIAGE* (1766)

Scene: An assembly.
Several persons at cards, at different tables; among the rest
Colonel Trill, Lord Minum, Mrs. Quaver, Sir Patrick Mahony.

(At the Quadrille Table)

COL. T.:	Ladies, with leave —
2nd LADY:	Pass!
3rd LADY:	Pass!
MRS. Q.:	You must do more.
COL. T.:	Indeed I can't.
MRS. Q.:	I play in hearts.
COL. T.:	Encore.
2nd LADY:	What luck?
COL. T.:	Tonight at Drury Lane is played

A comedy, and *toute nouvelle* — a spade!.
Is not Miss Crotchet at the play?

MRS. Q.:   My niece   5
Has made a party, sir, to damn the piece.

(At the Whist Table)

LORD M.:	I hate a playhouse. Trump! It makes me sick.
1st LADY:	We're two by honours, Ma'am.
LORD M.:	And we the odd trick.

Pray do you know the author, Colonel Trill?

COL. T.: I know no poets, heaven by praised! Spadille!   10
1st LADY: I'll tell you who, my Lord. *(Whispers my Lord)*
LORD M.:   What, he again!
And dwell such daring souls in little men?
Be whose it will, they down our throats will cram it.
COL. T.: O, no — I have a club — the best — we'll damn it.
MRS. Q.: O, bravo, colonel! Music is my flame.   15
LORD M.: And mine, by Jupiter! — We've won the game.
COL. T.: What, do you love all music?

MRS. Q.:   No, not Handel's.
              And nasty plays —
                              Are fit for Goths and Vandals.
                    (Rise from the table and pay)

                    (From the Piquet Table)
SIR P.:   Well, faith and troth, that Shakespeare was no fool!
COL. T.:   I'm glad you like him, sir. So ends the pool.   20
                    (Pay and rise from table)

                    (SONG — by the Colonel)
              I hate all their nonsense,
                    Their Shakespeares and Jonsons,
              Their plays and their playhouse and bards.
                    'Tis singing, not saying —
                    A fig for all playing —   25
              But playing, as we do, at cards.

                    I love to see Jonas,
                    Am pleased too with Comus —
              Each well the spectator rewards;
                    So clever, so neat in   30
                    Their tricks and their cheating —
              Like them we would fain deal our cards.

SIR P.:   King Lare is touching and how fine to see
              Ould Hamlet's ghost — "To be, or not to be".
              What are your operas to Othello's roar?   35
              Oh, he's an angel of a blackamoor!
LORD M.:   What, when he chokes his wife?
COL.T: And calls her whore?
SIR P.:   King Richard calls his horse and then Macbeth,
              Whene'er he murders, takes away the breath.
              My blood runs cold at every syllable,   40
              To see the dagger that's invisible. *(All laugh)*
              Laugh if you please. A pretty play —
LORD M.:   Is pretty.
SIR P.:   And when there's wit in't —
COL. T.:   To be sure, 'tis witty.
SIR P.:   I love the playhouse now — so light and gay
              With all those candles they have ta'en away.
                              (All laugh)   45

	For all your game, what makes it so much brighter?	
COL. T.:	Put out the light and then —	
LORD M.:	'Tis so much lighter.	
SIR P.:	Pray, do you mane, sirs, more than you express?	
COL. T.:	Just as it happens —	
LORD M.:	Either more or less.	
MRS. Q.:	Aren't you ashamed, sir? *(To Sir Patrick)*	
SIR P. :	Me! I seldom blush.	50
	For little Shakespeare, faith, I'd take a push.	
LORD M.:	News, news! Here comes Miss Crotchet from the play.	
	(Enter Miss Crotchet)	
MRS. Q.:	Well, Crotchet, what's the news?	
MISS C.:	We've lost the day.	
COL. T.:	Tell us, dear Miss, all you have heard and seen.	
MISS C.:	I'm tired — a chair — here, take my capuchin.	55
LORD M.:	And isn't it damned, Miss?	
MISS C.:	No, my Lord, not quite.	
	But we shall damn it.	
COL. T.:	When?	
MISS C.:	Tomorrow night.	

There is a party of us, all of fashion,
Resolved to exterminate this vulgar passion.
A playhouse — what a place! I must forswear it.   60
A little mischief only makes one bear it.
Such crowds of city folks, so rude and pressing!
And their horse-laughs so hideously distressing!
Whene'er we hissed they frowned and fell a-swearing,
Like their own Guildhall giants fierce and staring. 65

COL. T.:	What said the folks of fashion? Were they cross?	
LORD M.:	The rest have no more judgment than my horse.	
MISS C.:	Lord Grimly swore 'twas execrable stuff.	

Says one, "Why so, my Lord?" My Lord took snuff.
In the first act Lord George began to doze,   70
And criticised the author through his nose;
So loud, indeed, that as his lordship snored,
The pit turned round and all the brutes encored.
Some lords, indeed, approved the author's jokes.

LORD M.:	We have among us, Miss, some foolish folks.	75
MISS C.:	Says poor Lord Simper, "Well, now to my mind,	

The piece is good." But he's both deaf and blind.

SIR P.:	Upon my soul, a very pretty story,
	And quality appears in all its glory.
	There was some merit in the piece, no doubt. 80
MISS C.:	O, to be sure — if one could find it out.
COL. T.:	But tell us, Miss, the subject of the play.
MISS C.:	Why, 'twas a marriage — yes — a marriage — stay —
	A lord, an aunt, two sisters and a merchant,
	A baronet, ten lawyers, a fat serjeant, 85
	Are all produced to talk with one another,
	And about something make a mighty pother.
	They all go in and out and to and fro,
	And talk and quarrel as they come and go;
	Then go to bed and then get up and then 90
	Scream, faint, scold, kiss and go to bed again.
	(All laugh)
	Such is the play. Your judgment? Never sham it.
COL. T.:	Oh, damn it!
MRS. Q.:	Damn it!
1st LADY:	Damn it!
MISS C.:	Damn it!
LORD M.:	Damn it!
SIR P.:	Well, faith, you speak your minds and I'll be free.
	Good night! This company's too good for me.
	(Going) 95
COL. T.:	Your judgment, dear Sir Patrick, makes us proud.
	(All laugh)
SIR P.:	Laugh if you please, but pray don't laugh too loud.
	(Exit)

(RECITATIVE)

| COL. T.: | Now the barbarian's gone, Miss, tune your tongue, |
| | And let us raise our spirits high with song. |

(RECITATIVE)

| MISS C.: | Colonel, *de tout mon coeur* — I've one *in petto*, 100 |
| | Which you shall join and make it a *duetto*. |

(RECITATIVE)

| LORD M.: | *Bella signora et amico mio,* |
| | I too will join and then we'll make a *trio*. |

COL. T.:   Come all and join the full-mouthed chorus,
              And drive all tragedy and comedy before us.   105
(All the company rise and advance to the front of the stage)

(AIR)

COL. T.:   Would you ever go to see a tragedy?
MISS C.:   Never, never.
COL. T.:   A comedy?
LORD M.:   Never, never.
                    Live for ever
              Tweedledum and Tweedledee!

COL. T.,
LORD M.
AND MISS
C.:   Live for ever
              Tweedledum and Tweedledee!

(CHORUS)
Would you ever go to see, etc. .

The text follows that published with the play, 1766.

   Garrick's satire in this epilogue of the fashionable enthusiasm for opera culminates in an operatic burlesque for which music was composed by François Hippolyte Barthélémon, a violinist and composer who had come to London from France in 1765. Barthélémon is now principally remembered for the tune he wrote to Ken's hymn "Awake my soul, and with the sun".

   The cast of the epilogue was as follows:

Lord Minum	Mr. Dodd
Colonel Trill	Mr. Vernon
Sir Patrick Mahoney	Mr. Moody
Miss Crotchet	Mrs. Abington
Mrs. Quaver	Mrs. Lee
First Lady	Mrs. Bradshaw
Second Lady	Miss Mills
Third Lady	Mrs. Dorman

40

EPITAPH ON JAMES QUIN (1766)

That tongue, which set the table on a roar,
And charmed the public ear, is heard no more.
Closed are those eyes, the harbingers of wit,
Which spake, before the tongue, what Shakespeare writ.
Cold is that hand, which, living, was stretched forth,   5
At friendship's call, to succour modest worth.
Here lies James Quin. Deign, reader, to be taught,
Whate'er thy strength of body, force of thought,
In nature's happiest mould however cast,
To this complexion thou must come at last.   10

The text is from Quin's monument in the Abbey, Bath.

Quin died on January 21st 1766.

On Quin, see also 1, 16, 36, 38.

41

sung by Mr. Vernon in the character of Cymon

You gave me last week a young linnet
  Shut up in a fine golden cage,
Yet how sad the poor thing was within it,
  Oh how did it flutter and rage!
      Then he moped and he pined   5
      That his wings were confined
Till I opened the door of his den;
      Then so merry was he,
      And because he was free,
He came to his cage back again.   10

The text follows that published with the play, 1767.

Cymon, a dramatic romance by Garrick, was first performed at Drury Lane on January 2nd 1767, with music composed by Michael Arne, son of Dr. Thomas Arne. The romance had its origin in Dryden's poem "Cymon and Iphigenia".

Cymon is a youth held captive by the enchantress Urganda, whose love for him is unreciprocated. Cymon sings this song in a successful attempt to persuade Urganda that he might look on her with more favour if she were to free him from captivity.

42

MRS. PRITCHARD'S FAREWELL EPILOGUE (1768)

The curtain dropped, my mimic life is past;
That scene of sleep and terror was my last.
Could I in such a scene my exit make,
When every real feeling is awake,
Which, beating here, superior to all art,   5
Bursts in full tides from a most grateful heart?

I now appear myself, distressed, dismayed,
More than in all the characters I've played.
In acted passion tears must seem to flow,
But I have that within that passeth show.   10
Before I go and this loved spot forsake,
What gratitude can give — my wishes — take:
Upon your hearts may no affliction prey
Which cannot by the stage be chased away;
And may the stage, to please each virtuous mind,   15
Grow every day more moral, more refined —
Refined from grossness not by foreign skill —
Weed out the poison but be English still.

To all my brethren whom I leave behind,
Still may your bounty, as to me, be kind.   20
To me for many years your favours flowed,
Humbly received, on small desert bestowed;
For which I feel what cannot be expressed —
Words are too weak — my tears must speak the rest.

The text follows that published in L1 EP (April 25-27, 1768), PA (April 27, 1768), AR (1768) and Kearsley. According to L1 EP, this was "taken down by the help of shorthand". It differs in a few details from that published in LC (April 26-28, 1768), LM (April 1768) and SM (April 1768), but has the support, at points of difference, of a Folger transcript with corrections in Garrick's hand and of an autograph in the possession of the Pierpoint Morgan Library, New York City, which is part of a letter to Mrs. Pritchard (Letters, No. 498). The transcript and autograph are drafts of the epilogue earlier than the published texts. In the autograph, Garrick has marked lines which may be omitted and has also given Mrs. Pritchard some alternative readings.

Mrs. Pritchard's last appearance on the stage, prior to her retirement at the age of 57, was on April 25th 1768, when she played one of her finest roles, Lady Macbeth, to Garrick's Macbeth. The "scene of sleep and terror" to which she refers *(Macbeth, V, i)*, is singled out for special praise by Thomas Davies in his account of her performance in this role:

> In exhibiting the last scene of Lady Macbeth, in which the terrors of a guilty conscience keep the mind broad awake while the body sleeps, Mrs. Pritchard's acting resembled those sudden flashes of lightning which more accurately discover the horrors of surrounding darkness.

(Davies, II, 188-89)

On this epilogue, see Introduction, p. xxi.

43

O RARE WARWICKSHIRE! (1769)

Ye Warwickshire lads and ye lasses,
See what at our Jubilee passes,
Come revel away, rejoice and be glad,
For the lad of all lads was a Warwickshire lad,
    Warwickshire lad,   5
    All be glad,
For the lad of all lads was a Warwickshire lad.

Be proud of the charms of your county,
Where Nature has lavished her bounty,
Where much she has given, and some to be spared,   10
For the bard of all bards was a Warwickshire bard,
    Warwickshire bard,
    Never paired,
For the bard of all bards was a Warwickshire bard.

Each shire has its different pleasures,   15
Each shire has its different treasures,
But to rare Warwickshire all must submit,
For the wit of all wits was a Warwickshire wit,
    Warwickshire wit,
    How he writ!
For the wit of all wits was a Warwickshire wit.   20

Old Ben, Thomas Otway, John Dryden
And half a score more we take pride in,
Of famous Will Congreve we boast too the skill,
But the Will of all Wills was a Warwickshire Will,   25
    Warwickshire Will,
    Matchless still,
For the Will of all Wills was a Warwickshire Will.

Our Shakespeare compared is to no man,
Nor Frenchman, nor Grecian, nor Roman,   30
Their swans are all geese to the Avon's sweet swan,
And the man of all men was a Warwickshire man,

Warwickshire man,
Avon's swan,
And the man of all men was a Warwickshire man.   35

As ven'son is very inviting,
To steal it our bard took delight in,
To make his friends merry he never was lag,
And the wag of all wags was a Warwickshire wag,
    Warwickshire wag,   40
    Ever brag,
For the wag of all wags was a Warwickshire wag.

There never was seen such a creature,
Of all she was worth he robbed Nature,
He took all her smiles and he took all her grief,   45
And the thief of all thieves was a Warwickshire thief,
    Warwickshire thief,
    He's the chief,
For the thief of all thieves was a Warwickshire thief.

The text, except for a correction in line 25, follows that printed in Shakespeare's
Garland. Being a Collection of New Songs, Ballads, Roundelays, Catches, Comic-
Serenatas, etc. Performed at the Jubilee at S[t]ratford upon Avon, *1769. The version of
the song printed by Elizabeth P. Stein in her edition of* The Jubilee *(in* Three Plays by
David Garrick, *New York, 1926, rpt. 1967) from the Kemble-Devonshire transcript in
the Huntington Library, lacks the third and fifth stanzas. The title used here comes from
this source, as does the correction in line 25.*

25   Shakespeare's Garland *reads* was Warwickshire Will.

A three-day Shakespeare Jubilee was held at Stratford-on-Avon in
September 1769, with Garrick as Steward. This song was sung at the Jubilee
and achieved immediate popularity. Its tune, composed by Charles Dibdin
and played at the Jubilee by the band of the Warwickshire Militia, was to
become the regimental quickstep of the Royal Warwickshire Regiment. The
song was included also in *The Jubilee*, an entertainment based on the
Stratford experience, which was first performed at Drury Lane on October
14th 1769 and ran for ninety-two consecutive nights.

44

EPILOGUE TO 'TIS WELL IT'S NO WORSE (1770)

spoken by Mr. King

Instead of an epilogue, round, smart and terse,
Let poor simple me, and in more simple verse,
Just handle the text — *It is well it's no worse.*

The brat of this night should you cherish and nurse,
And hush it and rock it, though you fill not his purse,   5
The Daddy will say that — *'Tis well it's no worse.*

Or should his strange fortune turn out the reverse,
That his pockets you fill, though his play you should curse,
Still our author will say — *It is well it's no worse.*

Should you put the poor bard and his brat in one hearse,   10
Yet give to the actors some praise not averse,
We comfort ourselves with — *'Tis well it's no worse.*

The town with each poet will push carte and tierce.
If the bard can so guard that his buff you don't pierce,
Though you pink him a little — *'Tis well it's no worse.*   15

Should the playhouse be full, though the critics so fierce,
The managers, actors and author asperse,
We shrug up our shoulders — *'Tis well it's no worse.*

But should you to damn be resolved, and perverse,
If quietly after from hence you disperse,   20
We wish you good-night and — *It's well it's no worse.*

*The text follows that published with the play, 1770, except that an additional stanza
(lines 10-12) has been included. This is included in the epilogue by* LC *(Dec. 1-4, 1770),*
SJC *(Dec. 1-4, 1770),* WEP *(Dec. 1-4, 1770),* L1 EP *(Dec. 3-5, 1770),* TCM *(Dec. 1770),*
TB *and* Kearsley. *It is a stanza which the author of the play may well have disliked, and
this could account for its omission from the text published with the play. The text of
the additional stanza is taken from* SJC.

'Tis Well It's No Worse, a comedy by Isaac Bickerstaffe, was first performed at Drury Lane on November 24th 1770. In the preface printed with the play, Bickerstaffe says that it derives from *El Escondido y la Tapada*, by the Spanish dramatist, Calderón de la Barca.

The comedy is concerned with the devious means by which Don Carlos, sought by the authorities for killing a man in a duel, is reconciled with Don Guzman, father of the man he has killed, and marries Aurora, the young lady who has been the occasion of the duel. Its two liveliest characters are both servants. One of these, Muskato, servant of Don Carlos, was played by King, the speaker of the epilogue.

45

EPILOGUE TO *THE WEST INDIAN* (1771)

spoken by Mrs. Abington

Confess, good folks, has not Miss Rusport shown
Strange whims for seventeen hundred seventy-one?
What, pawn her jewels — there's a precious plan —
To extricate from want a brave *old* man!
And fall in love with poverty and honour —   5
A girl of fortune, fashion — fie upon her!
But do ñot think we females of the stage
So dead to the refinements of the age
That we agree with our old-fashioned poet;
I am point-blank against him and I'll show it.   10
And that my tongue may more politely run,
Make me a lady — Lady Blabington.
Now, with a rank and title to be free,
I'll make a catechism and you shall see
What is the *veritable baume de vie.*   15
As I change place I stand for that or this;
My Lady questions first, then answers Miss.
                    (She speaks as my Lady)
"Come, tell me, child, what were our modes and dress
In those strange times of that old fright Queen Bess?"
And now for Miss: *(She changes place and speaks for Miss)*
                    When Bess was England's queen,   20
Ladies were dismal beings, seldom seen.
They rose betimes and breakfasted as soon
On beef and beer, then studied Greek till noon.
Unpainted cheeks with blush of health did glow.
Beruffed and farthingaled from top to toe,   25
Nor necks nor ankles would they ever show.

Learnt Greek! *(Laughs)* Our outside head takes half a day.
Have we much time to dress the inside, pray?
No heads dressed *à la Grecque* the ancients quote —

112

There may be learning in a papillote. 30
Cards are our classics, and I, Lady B.,
In learning will not yield to any she
Of the late-founded female university.
But now for Lady Blab: *(Speaks as my Lady)*
                    "Tell me, Miss Nancy,
What sports and what employments did they fancy?" 35
                    (Speaks as Miss)
The vulgar creatures seldom left their houses,
But taught their children, worked, and loved their spouses;
The use of cards at Christmas only knew —
They played for little, and their games were few:
One-and-thirty, put, all fours and lantera loo. 40
They bore a race of mortals stout and bony,
And never heard the name of macaroni.
                    (Speaks as my Lady)
"Oh brava, brava — that's my pretty dear!
Now let a modern, modish fair appear.
No more of these old dowdy maids and wives — 45
Tell how superior beings pass their lives."
                    (Speaks as Miss)
Till noon they sleep, from noon till night they dress,
From night till morn they game it more or less;
Next night the same sweet course of joy run o'er,
Then the night after as the night before, 50
And the night after that, encore, encore.
                    (She comes forward)
Thus with our cards we shuffle off all sorrow,
Tomorrow and tomorrow and tomorrow.
We deal apace, from youth unto our prime,
To the last moment of our tabby-time; 55
And all our yesterdays, from rout and drum,
Have lighted fools with empty pockets home.
Thus do our lives with rapture roll away,
Not with the nonsense of our author's play.
This is true life, true spirit — give it praise, 60
Don't snarl and sigh for good Queen Bess's days.
For all you look so sour and bend the brow,
You all rejoice with me you're living now.

The text follows that published with the play, 1771.

The West Indian, a comedy by Richard Cumberland, was first performed at Drury Lane on January 19th 1771.

The Miss Rusport whom Mrs. Abington affects to mock, is the character she has just been acting. In the play, Miss Rusport, who is to inherit a substantial fortune when she comes of age, falls in love with a supposedly poor young man. She pawns her jewels to supply the needs of his father.

The play's title gave rise to the expectation that it would be a satire on West Indian merchants, so that a large number of those connected with the West Indies trade came to the opening performance. Garrick, indeed, remarked to Cumberland that the appearance of the house was more hostile than he had ever seen it (Cumberland, I, 295). But hostility melted as it became clear that Belcour, the "West Indian" in question, was to be shown in a favourable light.

Cumberland's play is a good example of the sentimental comedy which flourished at this time. Sentimental comedy moved people to tears rather than laughter. Characterization and plot were subservient to the necessity of a moral ending — Belcour, for instance, though something of a libertine, has a heart of gold, and O'Flaherty, the Irish major, scheming to marry a rich widow, proves generous, honest and chivalrous. Dialogue tended to sententiousness — "I am the offspring of distress," remarks Belcour, "and every child of sorrow is my brother; while I have hands to hold, therefore, I will hold them open to mankind." (Act I, sc. v)

On sentimental comedy see also 47.

46

EPILOGUE TO *ALONZO* (1773)

spoken by Mrs. Barry

Though lately dead, a princess and of Spain,
I am no ghost but flesh and blood again.
No time to change this dress — it is expedient
I pass for British and your most obedient.

How happy, ladies, for us all, that we   5
Born in this isle, by Magna Charta free,
Are not, like Spanish wives, kept under lock and key.
The Spaniard now is not like him of yore,
Who in his whiskered face his titles bore.
Nor joy nor vengeance made him smile or grin;   10
Fixed were his features, though the devil within.
He when once jealous, to wash out the stain,
Stalked home, stabbed madam and stalked out again.
Thanks to the times, this dagger-drawing passion
Through polished Europe is quite out of fashion.   15
Signor the Italian, quick of sight and hearing,
Once ever listening and for ever leering,
To *cara sposa* now politely kind,
He, best of husbands, is both deaf and blind.
Mynheer the Dutchman, with his sober pace,   20
Whene'er he finds his rib has wanted grace,
He feels no branches sprouting from his brain,
But calculation makes of loss and gain;
And when to part with her occasion's ripe,
Mynheer turns out mine frow and smokes his pipe.   25
When a brisk Frenchman's wife is given to prancing,
It never spoils his singing or his dancing:
"Madame, you false — *de tout mon coeur* — adieu;
Begar, you cocu me, I cocu you!"
He, *toujours gai*, dispels each jealous vapour,   30
Takes snuff, sings *Vive l'amour!* and cuts a caper.

As for John Bull — not he in upper life,
But the plain Englishman who loves his wife;
When honest John, I say, has got his doubts,
He sullen grows, scratches his head and pouts.   35
What is the matter with you, love? cries she;
Are you not well, my dearest? "Humph!" cries he.
You're such a brute! But, Mr. Bull, I've done.
"And if I am a brute, who made me one?"
You know my tenderness. My heart's too full!   40
"And so's my head — I thank you, Mrs. Bull."
O, you base man! "Zounds! madam, there's no bearing."
She falls a-weeping and he falls a-swearing.
With tears and oaths the storm domestic ends,
The thunder dies away, the rain descends;   45
She sobs, he melts, and then they kiss and friends.
Whatever ease these modern modes may bring,
A little jealousy is no bad thing.
To me, who speak from nature unrefined,
Jealousy is the bellows of the mind.   50
Touch it but gently and it warms desire;
If handled roughly you are all on fire;
If it stands still, affection must expire.
This truth no true philospher can doubt.
Whate'er you do, let not the flame go out.   55

The text follows that published with the play, 1773.

   Alonzo, a tragedy by John Home, was first performed at Drury Lane on
February 27th 1773.

   The tragedy is set in Spain. Alonzo, returning from eighteen years of
banishment, mistakenly accuses Ormisinda, whom he has secretly married just
before his banishment, of adultery. Alberto, who comes to her defence, is,
unknown to Alonzo, his own son. Ormisinda, who was played by Mrs. Barry,
dies after stabbing herself in an attempt to prevent father and son from
fighting. Alonzo, now convinced of her innocence, kills himself.

   Home had established his reputation as a dramatist with his tragedy
Douglas, which had had its first English performance at Covent Garden on
March 14th 1757, after having been rejected by Garrick. His association with
the theatre had forced Home to resign his ministry in the Church of Scotland.

47

PROLOGUE TO *SHE STOOPS TO CONQUER* (1773)

spoken by Mr. Woodward

Enter Mr. Woodward, dressed in black and holding a handkerchief to his eyes.

Excuse me, sirs, I pray, I can't yet speak —
I'm crying now, and have been all the week.
'Tis not alone this mourning suit, good masters;
I've that within for which there are no plasters.
Pray would you know the reason why I'm crying?   5
The comic muse, long sick, is now a-dying.
And if she goes, my tears will never stop,
For as a player I can't squeeze out one drop.
I am undone, that's all, shall lose my bread —
I'd rather, but that's nothing, lose my head.   10
When the sweet maid is laid upon the bier,
Shuter and I shall be chief mourners here.
To her a mawkish drab, of spurious breed,
Who deals in sentimentals, will succeed.
Poor Ned and I are dead to all intents —   15
We can as soon speak Greek as sentiments.
Both nervous grown, to keep our spirits up,
We now and then take down a hearty cup.
What shall we do? If Comedy forsake us,
They'll turn us out, and no one else will take us.   20
But why can't I be moral? Let me try.
My heart thus pressing, fixed my face and eye,
With a sententious look that nothing means
(Faces are blocks in sentimental scenes),
Thus I begin — *All is not gold that glitters;*   25
Pleasure seems sweet but proves a glass of bitters.
When ignorance enters, folly is at hand;
Learning is better far than house and land.

Let not your virtue trip, who trips may stumble;
And virtue is not virtue if she tumble.   30

I give it up — morals won't do for me;
To make you laugh I must play tragedy.
One hope remains. Hearing the maid was ill,
A doctor comes this night to show his skill.
To cheer her heart and give your muscles motion,   35
He, in five draughts prepared, presents a potion —
A kind of magic charm, for be assured,
If you will swallow it the maid is cured.
But desperate the doctor and her case is,
If you reject the dose and make wry faces.   40
This truth he boasts, will boast it while he lives,
No poisonous drugs are mixed in what he gives.
Should he succeed, you'll give him his degree;
If not, within he will receive no fee.
The college — *you* — must his pretensions back,   45
Pronounce him regular or dub him quack.

The text follows that published with the play, 1773.

She Stoops to Conquer, a comedy by Oliver Goldsmith, was first performed at Covent Garden on March 15th 1773.

On sentimental comedy, of which this prologue makes fun, see the commentary on 45. Garrick had also made fun of sentimental comedy in an earlier prologue, to which this one is obviously indebted. His prologue to Hugh Kelly's sentimental comedy *False Delicacy*, first performed at Drury Lane on January 23rd 1768, begins with the speaker, Thomas King, expressing his astonishment at the play that is to follow:

> I'm vexed, quite vexed, and you'll be vexed — that's worse;
> To deal with stubborn scribblers — there's the curse.
> Write moral plays — the blockhead! — why, good people,
> You'll soon expect this house to wear a steeple.
> For our fine piece, to let you into facts,
> Is quite a sermon, only preached in acts.
> You'll scarce believe me, till the proof appears,
> But even I, Tom Fool, must shed some tears.
> Do, ladies, look upon me — nay, no simpering —
> Think you this face was ever made for whimpering?
> Can I, a cambric handkerchief display,
> Thump my unfeeling breast and roar away?
>
> (Printed with the play, 1768)

More recently, on February 15th 1773, Samuel Foote had burlesqued sentimental comedy at his Haymarket theatre in a puppet-show entitled "The Handsome Housemaid, or Piety in Pattens". Public taste, however, clearly favoured sentimental comedy and there was some doubt whether Goldsmith's "laughing comedy", as he called it (see his "Essay on the Theatre; or a Comparison of Laughing and Sentimental Comedy", Goldsmith's *Works*, II, 209-13), would get a favourable reception. Goldsmith, however, had his enthusiastic supporters, amongst whom was Dr. Samuel Johnson. If Richard Cumberland is to be trusted (Cumberland, I, 366-69), Johnson was the leader of a band of well-wishers who dispersed themselves throughout the theatre on the play's opening night and applauded to pre-arranged signals. Goldsmith's comedy proved capable of succeeding through its own merits, however. By August 1773, it had not only been performed in various parts of England, but it had reached Dublin, Paris and even New York.

Woodward draws attention to his "mourning suit" (line 3). It was usual for the speaker of a prologue to dress in black. *The Spouter's Companion* (p. 89) prints a "Prologue upon Epilogues" which begins:

> *Enter in a black coat closely buttoned.*
>
> Behold me in the usual prologue dress,
> Though why it should be black, I cannot guess;
> Custom, the law of fools, improvement's foe,
> Has long established that it shall be so.
> But say, is slavish custom to control
> The active vigour of my free-born soul?
> I'll break the statutes and her laws deface —
> *(Unbuttoning his coat and displaying a gold-laced waistcoat)*
> Behold the glare of deviating lace; . . .

Woodward's attire was presumably more specifically appropriate to mourning than was "the usual prologue dress", however. This is borne out, not merely by line 3, but by Thomas Davies's explicit comment:

> "Woodward spoke this whimsical address in mourning . . ."
> (Davies, II, 157).

Woodward had no part in the play that was to follow. Edward Shuter, whose fondness for "a hearty cup" (line 18) was notorious, played the part of Hardcastle, whose house is mistaken for an inn, and himself for the landlord, by his daughter's prospective husband.

On Goldsmith (1728-74), whose medical qualifications provide matter for a joke (lines 34 ff.), see also 48.

48

JUPITER AND MERCURY (Late 1773 or early 1774)

Here, Hermes, says Jove, who with nectar was mellow,
Go fetch me some clay — I will make an odd fellow.
Right and wrong shall be jumbled, much gold and some dross.
Without cause be he pleased, without cause be he cross.
Be sure as I work to throw in contradictions —   5
A great love of truth, yet a mind turned to fictions.
Now mix these ingredients, which, warmed in the baking,
Turn to learning and gaming, religion and raking.
With the love of a wench, let his writings be chaste;
Tip his tongue with strange matter, his pen with fine taste;   10
That the rake and the poet o'er all may prevail,
Set fire to the head and set fire to the tail.
For the joy of each sex on the world I'll bestow it,
This scholar, rake, Christian, dupe, gamester and poet.
Though a mixture so odd, he shall merit great fame,   15
And among brother mortals be Goldsmith his name.
When on earth this strange meteor no more shall appear,
You, Hermes, shall fetch him to make us sport here.

The text follows that published in WEP *(Dec. 9-11, 1777) and* AR *(1777).*

"Jupiter and Mercury" was written in response to Goldsmith's poem *Retaliation*. Goldsmith's poem incorporates a series of mock epitaphs on members of the Club. This was the Club founded by Sir Joshua Reynolds and Dr. Johnson in 1764, of which Goldsmith was one of the original members, and to which Garrick was admitted in 1773. *Retaliation* was still unfinished at Goldsmith's death on April 4th 1774, but parts of it, including a mock epitaph on Garrick, had been circulated already. *Retaliation*, as the title suggests, was itself a response to a number of mock epitaphs which other members of the Club had composed for Goldsmith. Amongst these was one composed extempore by Garrick (see Introduction, p. xii).

On Goldsmith, see also 47.

49

EPILOGUE TO *THE MAID OF THE OAKS* (1774)

spoken by Mrs. Abington

In Parliament, whene'er a question comes
Which makes the Chief look grave and bite his thumbs,
A knowing one is sent, sly as a mouse,
To peep into the humour of the House.
I am that mouse, peeping at friends and foes,   5
To find which carry it, the Ayes or Noes.
With more than power of Parliament you sit,
Despotic representatives of wit,
For in a moment and without much pother,
You can dissolve this piece and call another.   10
As 'tis no treason, let us frankly see
In what they differ and in what agree,
The said supreme assembly of the nation,
With this our great dramatic convocation.
Business in both oft meets with interruption;   15
In both, we trust, no bribery or corruption;
Both, proud of freedom, have a turn to riot,
And the best Speaker cannot keep you quiet.
Nay, there as here, he knows not how to steer him,
When, "Order, order!" 's drowned in "Hear him, hear him!"   20
We have, unlike to them, one constant rule:
We open doors and choose our galleries full.
For a full house both send abroad their summons;
With us together sit the Lords and Commons.
You ladies here have votes, debate, dispute.   25
There if you go (oh, fie for shame!) you're mute.
Never was heard of such a persecution;
'Tis the great blemish of the constitution.
No human laws should nature's rights abridge,
Freedom of speech our dearest privilege.   30
Ours is the wiser sex, though deemed the weaker.
I'll put the question if you choose me Speaker.

Suppose me now bewigged and seated here.
I call to order; you: "The chair, the chair!"
Is it your pleasure that this bill should pass,   35
Which grants this poet, upon Mount Parnass,
A certain spot where never grew or corn or grass?

You that would pass this play, say "Aye" and save it;
You that say "No" would damn it. The Ayes have it.

---

*The text follows that published with the play, 1774, which is verbally identical with that
published with Burgoyne's* Works, 1808. *There seems no reason to doubt that this is the
version of the epilogue at which Garrick finally arrived after his many revisions, to which
the two Folger autographs, the Huntington transcript and the various printed versions
bear ample testimony.*

34. *The meaning is clearer in the Folger autographs, one of which reads:*
     I call to order — you call Chair, the Chair.

The Maid of the Oaks, a dramatic entertainment by John Burgoyne,
had its first performance at Drury Lane on November 5th 1774. It was based
on a *fête champêtre* which Burgoyne had organized to commemorate the
marriage of his wife's nephew, Lord Stanley, and Lady Betty Hamilton. The
fête champêtre had taken place on June 9th 1774 at "The Oaks", Lord
Stanley's residence near Epsom, Surrey.

Mrs. Abington played the part of Lady Bab in the entertainment. She
and Dupely, who imagines himself a lady-killer, have both been invited to a
country wedding, and Lady Bab is going to take part in the festivities dressed
as a shepherdess. She uses this disguise as a means of ridiculing Dupely, who
makes love to her under the impression that she really is a shepherdess. Mrs.
Abington took full advantage of the opportunity presented to her to display
her versatility in the quick transition from elegant lady to simple shepherdess.

John Burgoyne had distinguished himself both as a member of the
House of Commons and as a soldier. His military career was to suffer a
setback, however, when, leading a campaign against the Americans, he was
forced to surrender to a numerically superior force at Saratoga. He
subsequently wrote several more plays, the most successful being *The Heiress*
(1786).

50

FROM THE SPANISH (1775)

For me my fair a wreath has wove,
Where rival flowers in union meet;
As oft she kissed this gift of love
Her breath gave sweetness to the sweet.

A bee within a damask rose
Had crept, the nectared dew to sip;
But lesser sweets the thief foregoes
And fixes on Louisa's lip.

There tasting all the bloom of spring,
Waked by the ripening breath of May,
The ungrateful spoiler left his sting
And with the honey fled away.

The text follows that published in Twiss's Travels.

Garrick's song was written for inclusion in Richard Twiss's *Travels through Portugal and Spain in 1772 and 1773*, London, 1775. It derives from a Spanish madrigal by Lewis Martin, which is printed by Twiss in his account of Spanish literature.

51

SIR ANTHONY BRANVILLE'S ADDRESS TO THE LADIES
(1776)

Ladies, before I go, will you allow
A most devoted slave to make his bow?
Brought to your bar, ye most angelic jury,
'Tis you shall try me for my amorous fury.
Have I been guilty, pray, of indecorum?   5
My ardours were so fierce I could not lower 'em.
Such raging passions I confess an evil;
In flesh and blood like mine they play the devil.
Bound on the rack of love poor I was laid,
Between two fires, a widow and a maid.   10
My heart, poor scorched dove, now pants for rest;
Where, ladies, shall the flutterer find a nest?
Take pity, fair ones, on the tortured thing,
Heal it and let it once more chirp and sing.
Yet to approach you were infatuation.   15
If souls like mine, so prone to inflammation,
Should meet your tinder hearts there would be conflagration.
Indeed, so prudent are most men of fashion,
They run no danger for they feel no passion.
Though fairest faces smile, they can defy 'em,   20
Though softest tongues should plead, they can deny 'em;
Mankind would cease but for such loving fools as I am.
When I amongst them with my ardours glow,
I'm Mount Vesuvius in the midst of snow.
Had I the power, and of each sex were ruler,   25
I'd warm the one and make the other cooler.
When I address the fair, no art can smother
The mutual flame we kindle in each other.
I'm now electrified — therefore expedient
To fly combustibles! Ladies, your obedient.   30

The text follows that published in WEP *(Feb. 22-24, 1776),* PA *(Feb. 24, 1776),* L1 EP

At the revival of Mrs. Sheridan's *The Discovery* at Drury Lane on January 20th 1776, Garrick, as Sir Anthony Branville, was the only survivor of the original cast. His "Address to the Ladies" served as an epilogue. See commentary on 34 and the Introduction, pp. xv-xvi.

52

EPILOGUE TO *THE RUNAWAY* (1776)

spoken by Miss Younge

Posthaste from Italy arrives my lover.
Shall I to you, good friends, my fears discover?
Should foreign modes his virtues mar and mangle,
And *caro sposo* prove Sir Dingle Dangle,
No sooner joined than separate we go.   5
Abroad, we never shall each other know;
At home, I mope above — he'll pick his teeth below.
In sweet domestic chat we ne'er shall mingle,
And, wedded though I am, shall still live single.
However modish, I detest this plan.   10
For me no mawkish creature, weak and wan:
He must be English and an English-*man*.
To Nature and his country false and blind,
Should Belville dare to twist his form and mind,
I will discard him, and, to Britain true,   15
A Briton choose — and, maybe, one of you.
Nay, don't be frightened, I am but in jest;
Freemen, in love or war, should ne'er be pressed.

If you would know my utmost expectation,
'Tis one unspoiled by travelled education,   20
With knowledge, taste, much kindness and some whim,
Good sense to govern me — and let me govern him.
Great love of me must keep his heart from roving,
Then I'll forgive him if he proves too loving.
If in these times I should be blessed by fate   25
With such a phoenix, such a matchless mate,
I will by kindness and some small discerning
Take care that Hymen's torch continues burning.
At weddings nowadays, the torch, thrown down,
Just makes a smoke, then stinks throughout the town.   30
No married puritan, I'll follow pleasure

And even the fashion, but in moderate measure;
I will of opera ecstasies partake,
Though I take snuff to keep myself awake;
No rampant plumes shall o'er my temples play,   35
Foretelling that my brains will fly away;
Nor from my head shall strange vagaries spring,
To show the soil can teem with everything.
No fruits, roots, greens, shall fill the ample space,
A kitchen garden to adorn my face.   40
No rocks shall there be seen, no windmill, fountain,
Nor curls, like guns set round, to guard the mountain.
O learn, ye fair, if this same madness spreads,
Not to hold up but to keep down your heads.
Be not misled by strange fantastic art,   45
But in your dress let Nature take some part.
Her skill alone a lasting power ensures,
And best can ornament such charms as yours.

The text follows that published with the play, 1776.

The Runaway, by Mrs. Hannah Cowley, was first performed at Drury Lane on February 15th 1776. It was Mrs. Cowley's first play, and Garrick had helped her with it.

The epilogue's account (lines 35 ff.) of the ornamental headgear currently in fashion with the ladies scarcely exaggerates the facts. Garrick took comic advantage of the fashion in the revival of Vanbrugh's *The Provoked Wife* on April 30th 1776. Carrots figured prominently in the head-dress he sported when, in the role of Sir John Brute, he disguised himself as a lady. On this fashion, see also 55.

Miss Younge's opening remarks in the epilogue relate to her role of Bella in the play. At the end of the play, Belville, Bella's lover, is on his way home from Italy.

53

PROLOGUE TO *THE SPLEEN* (1776)

spoken by Mr. King

Though prologues now, as blackberries, are plenty,
And like them mawkish too, nineteen in twenty,
Yet you will have them when their date is o'er,
And "Prologue! Prologue!" still your honours roar,
Till some such dismal phiz as mine comes on: 5
"Ladies and gentlemen, indeed there's none;
The prologue, author, speaker, all are dead and gone."
These reasons have some weight and stop the rout;
You clap, I smirk — and thus go cringing out.
While living call me, for your pleasure use me;   10
Should I tip off, I hope you'll then excuse me.

So much for prologues — and now enter farce!
Shall I a scene I lately heard rehearse?
The place, the park; the dramatis personae,
Two female wits, with each a macaroni.   15
"Prithee, Lord Flimsey, what's this thing at Drury,
This *Spleen*?" — " 'Tis low, damned low, Ma'am, I assure ye."
"*C'est vrai*, my Lor', we now feel no such evil,
Never are haunted with a vapourish devil.
In pleasure's round we whirl it from the brain —   20
You rattle it away with *Seven's the main!*
In upper life we have no spleen or gall;
And as for other life, it is no life at all."

What can I say in our poor bard's behalf?
He hopes that lower life may make you laugh.   25
May not a trader who shall business drop,
Quitting at once his old accustomed shop,
In fancy through a course of pleasure run,
Retiring to his seat at Islington?
And of false dreams of happiness brimful,   30
Be at his villa miserably dull?

Would not he Islington's fine air forego,
Could he again be choked in Butcher Row,
In showing cloth renew his former pleasure,
Surpassed by none but that of clipping measure?   35
The master of this shop, too, seeks repose,
Sells off his stock in trade, his verse and prose,
His daggers, buskins, thunder, lightning and old clothes.
Will he in rural shades find ease and quiet?
Oh no, he'll sigh for Drury and seek peace in riot!   40

Nature of yore prevailed through human kind;
To low and middle life she's now confined.
'Twas there the choicest dramatists have sought her;
'Twas there Molière, there Jonson, Shakespeare caught her.
Then let our gleaning bard with safety come,   45
To pick up straws dropped from their harvest home.

The text follows that published with the play, 1776.

10-11. Kearsley and several periodicals say that these lines were omitted in performance.

The Spleen, a farce by George Colman, was first performed at Drury Lane on March 7th 1776.

The spleen was thought to be the seat of ill-humour, and so a bout of melancholia was known by that name. The "vapours" (see line 19) was another way of describing it. It is D'Oyley, a former draper, who suffers from the affliction in this play. In his retirement he has gone to live in Islington, which in those days was popular with London citizens for its fields and fresh air and for its health-giving waters.

Garrick's own impending retirement, mentioned in this epilogue (lines 36 ff.), was already public knowledge. *The Gentleman's Magazine* had in January carried a report that he was selling his share in Drury Lane.

54

AN OCCASIONAL PROLOGUE, SPOKEN BY MR. GARRICK
THE LAST TIME OF HIS PERFORMING, TOWARDS
INCREASING A FUND FOR THE RELIEF OF THOSE WHO,
FROM THEIR INFIRMITIES, SHALL BE OBLIGED TO
RETIRE FROM THE STAGE (1776)

A veteran see, whose last act on the stage
Entreats your smiles for sickness and for age?
Their cause I plead — plead it in heart and mind;
A fellow-feeling makes one wondrous kind.
Might we but hope your zeal would not be less,   5
When I am gone, to patronise distress;
That hope obtained the wished-for end secures,
To soothe their cares who oft have lightened yours.
Shall the great heroes of celestial line,
Who drank full bowls of Greek and Roman wine,   10
Caesar and Brutus, Agamemnon, Hector,
Nay, Jove himself, who here has quaffed his nectar —
Shall they, who governed Fortune, cringe and court her,
Thirst in their age and call in vain for porter;
Like Belisarius, tax the pitying street,   15
With *Date obolum* to all they meet?
Shan't I, who oft have drenched my hands in gore,
Stabbed many, poisoned some, beheaded more,
Who numbers slew in battle on this plain —
Shan't I, the slayer, try to feed the slain?   20
Brother to all, with equal love I view
The men who slew me and the men I slew.
I must, I will this happy project seize,
That those too old to die may live with ease.
Suppose the babes I smothered in the Tower   25
By chance or sickness lose their acting power —
Shall they, once princes, worse than all be served,
In childhood murdered and, when murdered, starved?
Matrons half-ravished for your recreation,
In age should never want some consolation.   30

Can I, young Hamlet once, to Nature lost,
Behold — O horrible! — my father's ghost,
With grisly beard, pale cheek, stalk up and down,
And he, the Royal Dane, want half-a-crown?
Forbid it, ladies; gentlemen, forbid it.   35
Give joy to age and let 'em say: "You did it."
To you, ye gods, I make my last appeal — *(To the upper gallery)*
You have a right to judge as well as feel.
Will your high wisdoms to our scheme incline,
That kings, queens, heroes, gods and ghosts may dine?   40
Olympus shakes — that omen all secures;
May every joy you give be ten-fold yours.

The text follows that published in LC *(June 15-18, 1776),* SJC *(June 15-18, 1776),* WEP *(June 15-18, 1776),* PA *(June 17, 1776),* L1 EP *(June 17-19, 1776),* LM *(June 1776),* SM *(June 1776),* UM *(June 1776),* WM *(June 1776),* GM *(July 1776),* AR *(1776),* CS *and Kearsley.*

Garrick regularly delivered a version of this prologue at benefit performances in aid of the Drury Lane fund for the relief of aged and infirm actors. A comparison of extant versions shows his continuing concern to improve his "Address" and to make it topical. The different endings employed to suit different occasions are of especial interest. A Folger transcript gives the endings used in 1766 (when Garrick played Kitely in Jonson's Every Man in His Humour), 1767 (when he played Ranger in Hoadly's The Suspicious Husband) and 1768 (when the address was evidently used as an epilogue):

1766:   Olympus Shakes — Earth Smiles — my heart sits lightly,
            The Act has pass'd — & now — I'll dress for Kitely.

1767:   Olympus shakes -- Earth Smiles — and what is Stranger
            I for this Scheme, at Fifty, — Dress for Ranger.

1768:   Olympus Shakes, Earth Smiles, nor Smiles in vain
            Here break we off, — next year, we'll come again
            With Grateful hearts your favours past remember
            So humbly take our Leaves till next September.

The ending employed in 1769, the year of the Shakespeare Jubilee at Stratford-upon-Avon, is also extant. This would follow naturally upon the 1768 ending. The text below follows PA *(May 23, 1769), except that the reading of the Folger autograph of these lines (see* Letters, *No. 538) has been adopted at line 6 (*our *for* the):

            My eyes, till then, no sight like this *(Bowing to the audience)* shall see,
            Unless we meet at Shakespeare's Jubilee.
            On Avon's banks, where flowers eternal blow,
            Like its full stream our gratitude should flow.
            There let us revel, show our fond regard,
            On that loved spot first breathed our matchless Bard.
            To him all honour, gratitude is due;
            To him we owe our all — to him and you!

A fund for the relief of aged and infirm actors had been started at

Drury Lane in the 1765-66 season. From 1766 on, a benefit performance was given at the end of every season in aid the this Theatrical Fund, in which Garrick always took part. In 1776 there were two such benefit performances — one on May 30th, and another, to which the present prologue belongs, on June 10th, when Garrick appeared for the last time on the Drury Lane stage.

Ill health persuaded Garrick to retire in his sixtieth year. During his final season he acted again many of his most famous roles. He had meant to end with Richard III, the role in which he had first made a name for himself, but decided that the strain of it would be more than he could bear on his final appearance. He chose, instead, to end his career as Don Felix, the jealous lover in Mrs. Susannah Centlivre's comedy *The Wonder*. The short speech which Garrick made at the end of the play began with an apology for his failure to speak the usual farewell epilogue:

> Ladies and Gentlemen,
> It has been customary with persons under my circumstances to address you in a farewell epilogue. I had the same intention, and turned my thoughts that way; but indeed I found myself *then* as incapable of writing such an epilogue as I should be *now* of speaking it.
>
> The jingle of rhyme and the language of fiction would but ill suit my present feelings . . . .

(Davies, II, 332-33)

55

PROLOGUE TO *A TRIP TO SCARBOROUGH* (1777)

spoken by Mr. King

What various transformations we remark
From east Whitechapel to the west Hyde Park.
Men, women, children, houses, signs and fashions,
State, stage, trade, taste, the humours and the passions;
The Exchange, Change Alley, wheresoe'er your ranging,   5
Court, city, country, all are changed or changing.
The streets, some time ago, were paved with stones,
Which, aided by a hackney coach, half broke your bones.
The purest lovers then indulged no bliss;
They run great hazard if they stole a kiss.   10
One chaste salute — the damsel cried "O fie!"
As they approached, slap went the coach awry.
Poor Sylvia got a bump and Damon a black eye.
But now weak nerves in hackney coaches roam,
And the crammed glutton snores, unjolted, home.   15
Of former times that polished thing a beau,
Is metamorphosed now from top to toe.
Then the full flaxen wig, spread o'er the shoulders,
Concealed the shallow head from the beholders.
But now the whole's reversed — each fop appears   20
Cropped and trimmed up, exposing head and ears.
The buckle then its modest limits knew;
Now, like the ocean, dreadful to the view,
Hath broke its bounds and swallows up the shoe.
The wearer's foot, like his once fine estate,   25
Is almost lost, the incumbrance is so great.
Ladies may smile. Are they not in the plot?
The bounds of nature have not they forgot?
Were they designed to be, when put together,
Made up, like shuttlecocks, of cork and feather?   30
Their pale-faced grandmammas appeared with grace
When dawning blushes rose upon the face.

No blushes now their once-loved station seek;
The foe is in possession of the cheek.
No head of old, too high in feathered state,   35
Hindered the fair to pass the lowest gate;
A church to enter now they must be bent,
If even they should try the experiment.

As change thus circulates throughout the nation,
Some plays may justly call for alteration,   40
At least to draw some slender covering o'er
That graceless wit which was too bare before.
Those writers well and wisely use their pens,
Who turn our wantons into Magdalens;
And howsoever wicked wits revile 'em,   45
We hope to find in you their stage asylum.

The text follows that published with the play, 1781.

38.   LC *(May 24-27, 1777), other journals and* TB *read* ever *for* even.

A Trip to Scarborough, a comedy by Richard Brinsley Sheridan,
Garrick's successor in the Drury Lane management, was first performed at
that theatre on February 24th 1777. It is an altered version of Sir John
Vanbrugh's *The Relapse*, and this leads Garrick to take change as the theme
of his prologue.

On the extravagant headgear worn by ladies at this time, see 52.

56

EPILOGUE TO *ALFRED* (1778)

spoken by Mrs. Barry

Our bards of late, so tragic in their calling,
Have scarce preserved one heroine from falling.
Whether the dame be widow, maid or wife,
She seldom from their hands escapes with life.
If this green cloth could speak, would it not tell   5
Upon its well-worn nap how oft I fell,
To death in various forms delivered up?
Steel kills me one night and the next the cup.
The tragic process is as short as certain;
With this *(she makes the motion of stabbing)* or this *(and here of*
       drinking poison), I drop, then drops the curtain.   10
No saint can lead a better life than I,
For half is spent in studying how to die.
The learn'd dispute how tragedies should end.
O happily, say some; some death defend.
Mild critics wish good fortune to the good;   15
While others, hot-brained, roar for blood, blood, blood.
The fair, though nervous, tragic to the soul,
Delights in daggers and the poisoned bowl:
"I would not give a black pin for a play,
Unless in tenderness I melt away.   20
From pangs and death no lovers would I save.
They should be wretched and despair and rave,
And ne'er together lie but in the grave."
The brave, rough soldier a soft heart discovers.
He swears and weeps at once, when dead the lovers.   25
As down his cheeks runs trickling nature's tide –
"Damn it! I wish those young ones had not died."
Though from his eyes the drop of pity falls,
He fights like Caesar when his country calls.
In spite of critic laws our bard takes part   30
And joins in concert with the soldier's heart.

O let your feelings with this party side —
For once forgive me that I have not died!
Too hard that fate which kills a virgin bride.

The text follows that published in L1 EP *(Feb. 13-16, 1778),* MC *(Feb. 16, 1778),* PA *(Feb. 17, 1778),* WEP *(Feb. 17-19, 1778),* GM *(Feb. 1778),* Lady's Magazine *(Feb. 1778),* SM *(Feb. 1778),* CS *and* TB. *It departs at one point from the text published with the play, 1778, which has the ungrammatical* run *(instead of* runs*) at line 26. The reading* runs *is confirmed by the two Folger autographs and the Huntington transcript.*

Alfred, a tragedy by John Home, was first performed at Covent Garden on January 21st 1778.

The play tells how Alfred, King of England, disguises himself as a bard and eventually rescues Ethelswida, his betrothed, who is a prisoner of the Danes. Mrs. Barry, speaker of the epilogue, played the part of Ethelswida.

57

**D.G. TO SQUIRE BALDWIN OF SHROPSHIRE, UPON HIS
COMPLAINING TO THE HOUSE THAT I WAS LET IN WHEN
ALL STRANGERS WERE EXCLUDED, AND THAT
I GLORIED IN MY SITUATION! (1778)**

Squire Baldwin rose with deep intent,
And notified to Parliament,
That I, it was a shame and sin,
When others were shut out, got in;
Asserting in his wise oration,   5
I gloried in my situation.
I own my features might betray
Peculiar joy I felt that day;
I glory when my mind is feasted
With dainties it has seldom tasted;   10
When reason chooses Fox's tongue
To be more rapid, clear and strong;
When from his classic urn Burke pours
A copious stream through banks of flowers;
When Barré stern, with accents deep,   15
Calls up Lord North and murders sleep;
And if his Lordship rise to speak,
Then wit and argument awake.
When Rigby speaks and all may hear him,
Who can withstand *ridendo verum?*   20
When Thurlow's words attention bind,
The spell's of a superior mind.
Now, whether I were Whig or Tory,
This was a time for me to glory.
My glory farther still extends,   25
For most of these I call my friends.
But if, Squire Baldwin, you were hurt
To see me, as you thought, so pert,
You might have punished my transgression,
And damped the ardour of expression.   30
A brute there is whose voice confounds

And frights all others with strange sounds;
Had you, your matchless powers displaying,
Like him, Squire Baldwin, set a-braying,
I should have lost all exultation,   35
Nor gloried in my situation.

The text follows that printed by Davies, which differs from Kearsley's text only at line 34, where Kearsley reads sat *for* set. *The reading* set *is confirmed by one of the two Folger autographs, which give earlier drafts of the poem. The only verbal departure from Davies's text is in the substitution of* Baldwin *for* B- n. Baldwin *is the reading of both the autographs. The title is taken from the later of the two autographs.*

    The occasion of these verses was a visit Garrick paid to the House of Commons in the spring of 1778. Because of a quarrel between two members of Parliament, the gallery was cleared of strangers, but Garrick, who had influential friends in the House, was allowed to remain. This led to a protest by Charles Baldwin (1729-1801), the member for Shropshire, who, says Garrick in a letter to Hannah More *(Letters*, No. 1184), "complained that a celebrated gentleman was admitted into the house when everybody else was excluded, and *that I gloried in my situation."* The whole house, Garrick goes on, "groaned at poor Baldwin, who is reckoned, par excellence, the dullest man in it." Hence Garrick, at the conclusion of his verses, compares Baldwin's speech to the braying of an ass.

    The number and distinction of those who rallied to Garrick's support was very gratifying to him, as were the sentiments they expressed. Burke enquired how they could possibly exclude from the hearing of their debates the great master of eloquence to whose example they were all indebted. Others followed in similar vein. "In short," Garrick concludes his account to Hannah More, "I am a much greater man than I thought."

58

ODE TO MUSIC
for the Catch Club (1778)

Hail Music, sweet enchantment, hail!
Like potent spells thy powers prevail;
On wings of rapture borne away,
All Nature owns thy universal sway.

For what is beauty, what is grace,   5
But harmony of form and face?
What are the beauties of the mind?
Heaven's rarest gifts, by harmony combined.

From the fierce passions discord springs,
Till Nature strike the softer strings;   10
The softer strings the soul compose,
And love, harmonious love, from passion flows.

Affection's flame and friendship's ties,
And all the social pleasures rise
From thee, O harmony divine!   15
Love, concord, beauty, every joy is thine.

The text follows SJC (May 26-28, 1778), MP (May 27, 1778), UM (June 1778), Kearsley and the Yale autograph. The autograph's division of the poem into stanzas is here adopted.

In 1778, the Noblemen's and Gentlemen's Catch Club offered a prize for the best glee composed to the words of this ode by Garrick. It was won by Samuel Webbe (1760-1816), who was to be winner of no less than twenty-seven of these annual Catch Club competitions. Garrick probably wrote the ode specially for the competition of 1778.

59

UPON MISS ARAB MORE DESIRING MY HANDWRITING FOR A BOOK IN WHICH SHE HAS COLLECTED THE HANDWRITING OF CELEBRATED MEN (1778)

In that choice book to wits devoted,
    And kept by you, my partial fair,
What, shall a name like mine be noted
    Among the various worthies there?

In that rare list I claim no place,   5
    Proud in your *mind* to fix my name,
While the true sons of genius grace
    The memorandum book of fame.

Yet I obey, if you command,
    Of Glory's page usurp a part,   10
For you have right to ask the hand
    Who have already got the heart.

The text is from Sotheby and Co.'s catalogue of June 18-21, 1928 (Lot 253).

"Arab" was a nickname for Martha ("Patty") More, a sister of Hannah More, authoress and close friend of the Garricks. Garrick's letter to Hannah More of November 23rd 1778 *(Letters,* No. 1209) appears to refer to these verses: "I have sent some nonsense to the Arab — dull truth without poetry — I forgot her Christian name, so have given the Mahometan one."

EXPLANATORY NOTES

Numbers refer to items of verse.

Shakespearean locations refer to the Arden editions of the plays, except in the cases of Hamlet *and* Richard III, *where references are to the New Cambridge editions.*

1. *Whitfield:* George Whitfield, or Whitefield (1714-70), one of the leaders of the Methodist movement.

2. *repetatur haustus:* the conventional Latin tag to indicate that a dose of medicine should be taken regularly.

4. *Bilked:* cheated. The monkey got into the boxes without paying the attendant.

5. *Dulcineas.* In Cervantes's *Don Quixote*, Dulcinea is the lady to whose service Don Quixote is dedicated.

playhouse guards. Military guards had been assigned to the patent theatres in 1721, following a riot at the theatre in Lincoln's Inn Fields (at that time functioning under royal patent). However, fear of public reaction and of the possible political consequences, if military force were to be used in a theatre, rendered the guards ineffective in preventing disturbances.

cuse: accuse, in the sense of "find fault with".

The jealous Moor: Shakespeare's Othello. Lines 34 to the end are a parody of *Othello*, III, iii, 351-63.

Deard sold trinkets in Pall Mall, London.

6. *Cry "Havoc!" and let slip the dogs of war:* from Shakespeare's *Julius Caesar,* III, i, 273.

Hamlet's mother: Mrs. Pritchard, who played this role in Shakespeare's tragedy.

the Cobbler's wife: Mrs. Clive, who played Nell, wife of Jobson the cobbler, in Charles Coffey's popular ballad opera *The Devil to Pay.*

Harlequin: the principal figure in the English pantomime of this period.

the vaulting Turk: the "Mahomet" of Johnson's 1747 prologue, a rope-dancer who had performed at Covent Garden.

7. *elections . . . Jews.* The current controversy about the Jews was connected with the recent Naturalization Act, which was soon to be repealed because of the public outcry against it. The act enabled foreign Jews to become naturalized British subjects after three years' residence, without having to take the Sacrament. It also endorsed the right of British Jews to hold land. There had been violent speeches on the matter in Parliament and much controversy in the press; public meetings were held, pamphlets written; it was even alleged that Jewish interests had bribed the government with half a million pounds. All this was partly occasioned by the fact that a general election was pending and the opposition was looking for an issue on which to stir up public feeling against the Pelham administration.

lotteries. Annual lotteries were held at this time and sanctioned by Act of Parliament. Irregularities were suspected in the allocation of tickets for the 1753 lottery and in December of that year a committee was set up by the House of Commons to investigate the matter.

Canning . . . Squires. The controversy surrounding Elizabeth Canning and Mary Squires was at its height when Foote spoke this prologue. Elizabeth Canning, an eighteen-years-old domestic servant, disappeared after visiting her uncle and aunt on New Year's day 1753. Returning home a month later in a miserable condition, half-starved and half-naked, she said she had been attacked by two men and carried off to a brothel, where she had been held prisoner until she escaped through a window. All she had had to eat were bread and butter and a mince-pie she had had in her pocket. The details she gave suggested an establishment kept by a certain "Mother" Wells at Enfield. The girl was taken there and said that she thought she recognized the attic where she had been held. She also picked out an old gypsy, Mary Squires, as the woman who had cut off her stays and thrust her into her prison. Squires and Wells were tried and found guilty. Wells was branded on the hand and sentenced to six months' imprisonment; Squires was sentenced to death. But Sir Crisp Gascoyne, Lord Mayor of London, who presided over the Old Bailey trial *ex officio*, was not satisfied with the verdict, and secured a stay of execution for Squires while further enquiries were made. His action aroused indignation in some quarters and many pamphlets were issued on both sides. In May of the following year, as a result of these enquiries, Canning was tried for perjury, found guilty, and sentenced to seven years' transportation. Squires was given a free pardon.

a fiddler's nose. Giacobbe Cervetto, who played the cello in the orchestra at Drury Lane, had a very large nose, and was also conspicuous because of the huge diamond he wore on his bow hand. The audience in the upper gallery was fond of shouting "Play up, Nosey!" The cry continued in use after Cervetto had left Drury Lane, and spread to other theatres as well. John Taylor (*Records of My Life,* London, 1832, I, 252) mentions its having been heard in a Nottingham theatre.

a hum: a piece of humbug.

8.   *vild:* dialectal variant of "vile".

nine days' abode. If a new play reached nine performances, it meant that the author had three benefits, one on the third, one on the sixth and one on the ninth night. Out of the takings he had to pay house charges — £60 a night at this time. *Virginia*, in fact, had eleven performances.

10.   *sea-toad.* The meat eaten by the boy's first master was turtle, a very fashionable delicacy at this time.

belly-patch: a reference to the "plastron" — that part of the shell of a turtle which protects its belly.

capapee (from Old French *de cap à pié*, from head to foot): an appropriate term because of the completeness of the protection afforded by the turtle's shell.

E'feck: in faith, truly.

11.   *to die, to sleep, no more: Hamlet*, III, i, 60-61. The "fine gentleman", in his ignorance, thinks that this quotation comes from an opera.

12.   *Locke:* John Locke (1632-1704), English philosopher, author of *An Essay concerning Human Understanding*, etc.

Newton: Sir Isaac Newton (1642-1727), English mathematician and scientist, the discoverer of differential calculus, the Law of universal gravitation, etc.

Boyle: Robert Boyle (1627-91), English scientist, the discoverer of Boyle's law concerning the compressibility of gases, and one of the founders of modern chemistry.

13.   *flip:* a mixture of beer and brandy, sweetened with sugar and heated.

sugar-plum: properly a confection made of boiled sugar, but the sailor refers by this name to his wad of chewing-tobacco.

Royal George: British naval flagship.

coxon: coxswain.

14.   *'tis here, 'tis there, 'tis gone.* Cf. *Hamlet*, I, i, 141-42.

The Greek-read critic. Neo-classical critics, especially those of France, claimed, with little justification, the authority of the Greek Aristotle (384-

322 B.C.) for their insistence that tragedy must observe the unities of *time and place* (see line 15), i.e. must confine its action to one place and to a period of time not much exceeding twenty-four hours.

Blood! Blood! Blood! Iago! Cf. *Othello*, III, iii, 458.

triumphs, funerals, coronations. This kind of spectacle had become very popular in the theatre. For instance, when *Romeo and Juliet* opened at Covent Garden on September 28th 1750 (see commentary on 6), a new scene had been introduced representing Juliet's funeral procession. On October 1st, Garrick responded by adding a funeral procession to his production of the play at Drury Lane.

Bossu (1631-80): French critic.

16. *He that is robbed, etc.: Othello,* III, iii, 348-49.

Jack Falstaff. Quin played the role of Falstaff in both parts of Shakespeare's *Henry IV* and also in his *Merry Wives of Windsor.* Cf. 38, line 24.

21. *routs:* fashionable social gatherings at which there was card-playing. See note on 45.

The ladies shall play crowns: "play" in the sense of "to wager in a game" *(O.E.D.,* s.v. Play, *v.* 21). The pretence is that the audience is being invited to play at cards. Five shillings was the price of a seat in a box.

shilling party: "party" in the sense of "a game or match" *(O.E.D.,* s.v. Party, *sb.* II, 10). A shilling party was where cards were played for stakes of a shilling. Cf. Muslin's remarks on Mrs. Marmalet in Act I of Arthur Murphy's *The Way to Keep Him:*

> How the devil does she think I can make a shilling party for her? There is no such thing nowadays; nobody plays shilling whist now, unless I was to invite the tradespeople.

One shilling was the price of admission to the upper gallery (cf. 8, line 9).

22. *Brussels Gazette.* This journal had a bad reputation in England. It was supposed to disseminate false information.

26. *Long before the beginning of the play:* a slight misquotation from a speech by *Bayes* (see line 38), the playwright who is the central character in *The Rehearsal,* a satirical play by George Villiers, Duke of Buckingham (1628-87). Bayes was one of Garrick's famous roles. In the speech in question, Bayes is trying to explain to a puzzled onlooker a quite incomprehensible scene from his new play:

> Why, Sir, you must know that, long before the beginning of this play, this prince was taken by a fisherman . . . .

A little flattery sometimes does well: a memorable "aside" spoken by Richard III (another of Garrick's famous roles) after he has been praising Buckingham in Act III of Colley Cibber's adaptation of Shakespeare's *Richard III.* See Introduction, p. xvii.

28.   *Hymen:* the god of marriage in Greek and Roman mythology.

29.   *Pam:* the knave of clubs, the highest trump in the card-game of *loo.*

Moll Peatly: the name of a dance.

30:   *strut and fret.* Cf. *Macbeth,* V, v, 25.

31:   *Ranelagh.* The gardens which Richard, Viscount Ranelagh, had laid out about 1690, were thrown open to the public, on a commercial basis, in 1742. They became very popular with fashionable society. There was a building called the Rotunda where concerts were held. On Friday, June 12th 1761, just three days before the première of *All in the Wrong,* there had been an ingenious and elaborate display of fireworks in the gardens and a performance of Congreve's masque *The Judgement of Paris,* with music composed by Dr. Thomas Arne. This was a benefit performance for *Ferdinando Tenducci,* who, like *John Beard,* also mentioned in this epilogue, was a leading singer of the day.

Vauxhall. Vauxhall Gardens had been opened to the public in 1661, and had soon become a favourite resort of the populace. They were a purely summer resort, and the usual method of reaching them was by water. An enclosed concert room had been erected there in 1758.

the famed winged steed: Pegasus, a mythological horse which brought into being, with the blow of a hoof, the fountain Hippocrene, a source of poetic inspiration, and is therefore sometimes thought of as bearing the poet in his flights of imagination.

32.   *brim:* a vicious woman (contraction of "brimstone").

Gossip Muse: In classical mythology the Muses are nine goddesses, all sisters, who are regarded as the inspirers of learning and the arts. Like a true epic poet, Garrick invokes the assistance of the Muse most appropriate to his requirements.

flea: an old form of "flay".

145

Panfribblerium: a council of all the fribbles, so called after "Pandaemonium, the high capital/Of Satan and his peers" (*Paradise Lost*, I, 756-757). The debate of the fribbles parodies that of the fallen angels in Book II of Milton's poem.

a place upon a hill: Hampstead, which, thanks to its supposedly medicinal waters and its fresh country air, had become a fashionable spa by the early eighteenth century. Dances and concerts like those mentioned in the lines that follow were, from the beginning of the century, amongst the entertainments provided.

ditto: the cloth in a suit of clothes where each item is of the same material.

once a week. Throughout the eighteenth century, Monday seems to have been the regular day for dances and assemblies during the summer season at Hampstead.

Johnny Beard. See note on 31.

jumps: the same as *fidgets* (line 174).

In forty-eight, . . . the month November. Garrick's memory is probably at fault here. There is no record of his having performed the part of Fribble during November 1748. *Miss in Her Teens,* with Garrick as Fribble, had its première at Covent Garden on January 17th 1747. Its first performance at Drury Lane was on October 24th 1747.

demi-reps: women of doubtful reputation (from "demi-reputable").

spinnet: a smaller version of the harpsichord. When the keys were pressed, the strings were plucked by means of quills.

Jack-my-Gills: effeminates, who are both Jack and Gill, male and female.

Blood, Mr. Fizgig, blood, blood, blood. See note on 14.

Salts, hartshorn, peppermint and eau-de-luce: smelling salts.

the patch upon his lip. Tiny pieces of black silk were often worn on the face, especially by women, for decoration or to hide a blemish.

Just published by a reverend wit. The descriptions of the actor as "a thing", a "merry-andrew, paper king" etc. derive from the Rev. Charles Churchill's *Apology addressed to the Critical Reviewers*, first published in May 1761. It was in this poem that Churchill asserted his authorship of *The Rosciad* (see lines 63-64 of *The Fribbleriad*) after the *Critical Review* had attributed it elsewhere.

like Polonius etc. The shapes which Hamlet persuades Polonius to see in a cloud (*Hamlet*, III, ii, 395-401) are those of a camel, a weasel and a whale. But in Garrick's day, Pope's emendation of "ousel" (= blackbird) for "weasel" was adopted. "There is humour," claims Lewis Theobald, in his note on this passage in his edition of Shakespeare (1734), "in comparing the same cloud to a beast, a bird, and a fish."

Scrub: in George Farquhar's comedy *The Beaux' Stratagem*, a role in which Garrick enjoyed great success.

barbers' blocks: stands for wigs.

Brutus: the friend of Julius Caesar, in Shakespeare's tragedy of that name, who is nevertheless persuaded to take part in his assassination.

33.   *routs.* See note on 21.

sugar-plums: sweetmeats.

35.   *Churchill.* See commentary on 32.

Shandy: the central character and narrator in Laurence Sterne's novel *Tristram Shandy*, the nine volumes of which were published between 1760 and 1767. Volumes seven and eight had appeared in January 1765, a few months before *The Sick Monkey* was published.

Chalkstone's Lord. The part of Lord Chalkstone, a gouty but spirited old gentleman, played by Garrick, had been added to his farce, *Lethe,* when it was revived in 1756.

Fribble: a character in Garrick's farce *Miss in Her Teens*. See commentary on 32.

The rugged Russian bear: Macbeth, III, iv, 99.

The little dogs and all: King Lear, III, vi, 62.

'Twere well it were done quickly: Macbeth, I, vii, 1-2.

The steed alone was firm and fast. The steed stands for George Colman — so Garrick says in the letter in which he first tells Colman of *The Sick Monkey (Letters,* No. 352).

megrim: migraine.

the spleen. See commentary on 53.

nostrums. According to *Letters*, No. 355, Garrick had particularly in mind Dr. John Hill, whose advertisements for quack medicines regularly appeared in the *Public Advertiser* and other newspapers. See commentary on 18.

Warwick Lane: where the College of Physicians was situated.

The wine was better than the bush. Cf. the proverb "Good wine needs no bush" (see Shakespeare, Epilogue to *As You Like It*). A branch was formerly hung out in front of a tavern as a sign that liquor was sold inside.

John *Radcliffe* (1650-1714) was a distinguished physician.

papilloted. A papillote was a paper for curling the hair.

Sir Wilful: in William Congreve's comedy *The Way of the World*.

37.   *Punchinello,* often shortened to "Punch", was already a popular figure in puppet shows. The puppet appears to have developed from a character in the *commedia dell'arte*. Pepys tells of hearing a fat child called "Punch" — "which pleased me mightily, that word being become a word of common use for all that is thick and short" *(Diary of Samuel Pepys,* ed. Robert Latham and William Matthews, London, 1976, IX, 538).

Sir John. Garrick never played the part of Shakespeare's Sir John Falstaff.

Chelsea pensioner. The Royal Hospital for invalid soldiers had been established in Chelsea since 1694.

38.   *struts his hour upon the stage.* Cf. *Macbeth*, V, v, 25.

39.   *Minum:* an old spelling of minim.

Spadille: the ace of spades in the game of quadrille.

and dwell such daring souls in little men? This is a slight misquotation from Pope, *The Rape of the Lock,* I, 11-12:

> And dwells such rage in softest bosoms then,
> And lodge such daring Souls in little Men?

The lines are from the first edition of Pope's poem and were subsequently changed. Both Garrick and Colman were conspicuously small in stature.

Goths and Vandals. Cf. Lord Ogleby's outburst in *The Clandestine Marriage* upon the vulgarity of the middle-class family into which his nephew proposes to marry: "I'll not be left among these Goths and Vandals, your Sterlings, your Heidelbergs, and Devilbergs" *(Dramatic Works of David Garrick*, 1798, rpt. London 1969, III, 51-52).

Jonas. I have not succeeded in tracing the character referred to.

Comus: a character in John Dalton's adaptation of Milton's masque of that name, which was set to music by Thomas Arne.

"To be or not to be": Hamlet, III, i, 56.

King Richard calls his horse: Richard III, V, iv, 7.

the dagger that's invisible: Macbeth, II, i, 33 ff.

all those candles they have ta'en away. This refers to the new stage lighting which Garrick had introduced at Drury Lane earlier that season. Previously there had been six chandeliers over the stage, with the naked flames of the candles visible to the audience and, no doubt, very trying to the eyes. Under the new system the source of light was concealed from view and much of it came from the side of the stage. Its strength and clarity were also improved.

Put out the light and then: Othello, V, ii, 7.

capuchin: a woman's cloak with a hood, based on the dress of Capuchin friars.

their horse-laughs. Cf. Mrs. Heidelberg's advice to her brother, Mr. Sterling, in *The Clandestine Marriage*, on how to behave in aristocratic company: "and don't burst out with your horrible loud horse-laughs. It is monstrous vulgar" *(Dramatic Works of David Garrick*, III, 16).

Guildhall giants: two giant figures of wood, known as Gog and Magog, at the Guildhall, the council hall of the Corporation of the City of London.

Why, 'twas a marriage, etc. The play which Miss Crotchet has been to see, and of which her recollections are already somewhat vague, is, of course, *The Clandestine Marriage*.

in petto: in reserve (Italian).

Tweedledum and Tweedledee. In the 1720s a rivalry had sprung up between the two composers Handel and Bononcini. This divided the music-loving public and occasioned the lines variously attributed to Pope, Swift and John Byrom:

Some say, compared to Bononcini,
That Mynheer Handel's but a ninny.
Others aver that he to Handel
Is scarcely fit to hold a candle.
Strange all this difference should be
'Twixt Tweedledum and Tweedledee.

40. *set the table on a roar: Hamlet,* V, i 185.

To this complexion thou must come. Cf. *Hamlet*, V, i, 188.

42. *But I have that within that passeth show.* Cf. *Hamlet*, I, ii, 85.

43. *Old Ben:* Ben Jonson (1573?-1637).

brag: lively.

44. *carte and tierce:* positions adopted in fencing, from which an attack can be made.

buff: leather worn for protection.

45. *veritable baume de vie.* The baume de vie was a much advertised patent medicine.

beruffed: wearing a ruff, or deep frilly collar.

farthingaled: wearing a hooped petticoat.

à la Grecque: Richard Carson suggests that hair styles at this time were influenced by the Greek revival in architecture *(Fashions in Hair, the first five thousand years,* 2nd rev. ed., London, 1971, p. 329).

lines 29-30: "If you dress your hair in the Greek style, you don't have time to acquire sufficient knowledge to quote the classics. The only learning that's involved is what's printed on the papers you use to curl your hair."

the late-founded female university: a reference to the mixed parties of men and women presided over by Mrs. Elizabeth Montagu and other London hostesses, at which card-playing was prohibited and the guests encouraged to discuss literary topics. Dr. Johnson said of Mrs. Montague: "She diffuses more knowledge in her conversation than any woman I know, or, indeed, almost any man" (see Boswell, IV, 275n).

One-and-thirty, put, all fours and lantera loo: all long-established card games.

macaroni: a dandy of the 1760s and 1770s. It would seem likely that this use of "macaroni" derived from an Italian usage mentioned by Addison, *Spectator*, No. 47. He refers to "those circumforaneous wits whom every nation calls by the name of that dish of meat which it loves best. In *Holland* they are termed *Pickled Herrings;* in *France, Jean Pottages;* in *Italy, Macaronies;* and in *Great Britain, Jack Puddings.*"

Tomorrow and tomorrow and tomorrow and lines following. Cf. *Macbeth*, V, v, 19 ff.

rout and drum. A drum, like a rout, was an evening party attended by people of fashion, at which cards were played. *O.E.D.* (s.v. Drum, *sb.*[1] 10) cites Eliza Heywood, *Female Spectator* (1748), II, 269:

> She told me, that, when the number of a company for play exceeded ten tables, it was called a *racquet;* if under, it was only a *rout*; and if no more than one or two, it was only a *drum.*

46. *He feels no branches sprouting from his brain.* A cuckold was supposed to sprout antlers on his forehead. Cf. line 41.

Begar: supposed to represent a Frenchman's pronunciation of "Begad" ("By God").

47. *'Tis not alone this mourning suit, good masters*, etc. Cf. *Hamlet*, I, ii, 77 ff.

blocks: barbers' blocks. See note on 32.

48. *Hermes* (or Mercury): the messenger of *Jove* (or Jupiter), the supreme deity of the Romans.

49. *Mount Parnass . . . where never grew or corn or grass.* In Greek mythology, Parnassus was regarded as the haunt of the Muses. Although it had groves conducive to meditation, its soil was barren. For Garrick, this signifies that successful authorship is not going to bring riches. An earlier draft of the epilogue in a Folger autograph expresses the thought more fully:

> Our Author claims a right (if his Bill pass),
> To half an acre upon Mount Parnass,
> Where plenty never on the owner pours;
> And where indeed are more of thorns than flow'rs.

52. *Sir Dingle Dangle.* The name suggests the character intended. A dangler was a man who hung around women, but lacked the ability to do any more than that. *The London Magazine and Monthly Chronicler* (Dublin) for September 1747 has some anonymous lines on the subject. They begin:

A Dangler is of neither sex,
A creature born to tease and vex:
A creature bred by intuition,
And satisfied without fruition.

Hymen. See note on 28.

opera ecstasies. See 39.

53.　*macaroni.* See note on 45.

Seven's the main! In the game of hazard, the player who is throwing the dice calls out a number between five and nine. This is "the main". If he throws it, he wins from the banker the sum played for.

Butcher Row: a slum street near Temple Bar in London, so called because butchers were amongst those who did business there.

Surpassed by none but that of clipping measure. The only pleasure greater than that of showing off his cloth to a customer is that of clipping it when he has made a sale.

buskins: thick-soled boots used by Greek tragic actors to increase their height.

54.　*Caesar and Brutus:* in Shakespeare's *Julius Caesar,* which had not, however, been performed at Drury Lane since April 30th 1747.

Agamemnon, Hector: in Shakespeare's *Troilus and Cressida,* which had last been performed at Drury Lane (in Dryden's adaptation) on June 2nd 1709. Agamemnon also appears in James Thomson's play of that name, which had last been performed at Drury Lane on April 25th 1738.

Jove himself: in Dryden's comedy *Amphitryon,* last performed at Drury Lane (in an adptation by Dr. John Hawkesworth) on May 20th 1774.

Belisarius: Byzantine general who, in his old age, fell into temporary disgrace when falsely accused of being involved in a plot against the life of Emperor Justinian. According to Edward Gibbon, the story "that he was deprived of his eyes, and reduced by envy to beg his bread, 'Give a penny to Belisarius the general!' is a fiction of later times, which has obtained credit, or rather favour, as a strange example of the vicissitudes of fortune" *(Decline and Fall of the Roman Empire,* ed. J.B. Bury, 4th ed., London, 1911, IV, 429-30).

Date obolum: Give a penny (Latin).

the babes I smothered in the Tower. As Richard III, in Shakespeare's tragedy of that name, Garrick was responsible for having the two young princes, his nephews, smothered in the Tower of London.

O horrible! Hamlet, I, v, 80.

To you, ye gods etc. Cf. Oedipus in Dryden and Lee's tragedy of that name, in his last speech of Act III:

> To you, good gods, I make my last appeal;
> Or clear my virtue, or my crime reveal.

Olympus: the upper gallery, considered the dwelling place of the gods because those who sit there are the ones whose opinion really matters. Their "nod" of approval is like the approval of Jove himself.

55. *The Exchange:* the Royal Exchange, situated between Cornhill and Threadneedle Street.

Change Alley: just below the Royal Exchange and leading from Cornhill into Lombard Street. The great fire in Cornhill of March 1748, which destroyed nearly a hundred houses, started in Change Alley.

run: old form of "ran".

graceless wit. Cf. Pope's comment on Vanbrugh, from whose comedy *The Relapse, A Trip to Scarborough* is adapted:

> How Van wants grace, who never wanted wit!
>
> *(Imitations of Horace,* II, i, 289)

Magdalens: Mary Magdalene, or Magdalen, the follower of Jesus, is supposed to have been a prostitute before her conversion. Magdalen asylums (see line 46) were for the reformation of prostitutes.

56. *this green cloth:* a cloth of green baize spread over the stage so that "corpses" who had to lie there did not dirty their clothes. This was especially for the sake of the usually magnificently dressed tragic heroines.

blood, blood, blood. See note on 14.

a black pin: a pin such as would be used in fastening up the black dress appropriate to a woman who liked to mourn.

57. *Fox.* Charles James Fox (1749-1806) was famous for his oratory. He had served both as a Lord of the Admiralty and a Lord of the Treasury, but

was out of office at this time, having incurred the displeasure of George III. Like Garrick, Fox was a member of "The Club" (see commentary on 48).

Burke. Edmund Burke (1729-97) was one of the most eloquent and powerful speakers in the House of Commons at this time. He, also, was a member of "The Club".

Barré. Isaac Barré (1726-1802) was an Irishman who had served as a soldier before entering Parliament in 1761. In the quarrel between the British Government and the American colonies, which had erupted into the American War of Independence, Barré was a consistent defender of the rights of the colonies.

Lord North (1732-92) was Prime Minister at this time.

murders sleep. Cf. *Macbeth*, II, ii, 35 ff.

Rigby. Richard Rigby (1722-88) held the office of Paymaster of the Forces.

ridendo verum: the truth through laughter (Latin) — i.e. Rigby presents the truth in an amusing way. Cf. Horace, *Satires,* I, i:

> quamquam ridentem dicere verum
> quid vetat?

("yet may not truth be spoken in laughing vein?")

Thurlow. Edward Thurlow (1731-1806) was Attorney General at this time.

SPEAKERS OF GARRICK'S PROLOGUES
AND EPILOGUES.

Frances Abington (1737-1815).

Mrs. Abington was the daughter of a cobbler and former private in the Guards. After making a living as a flower-girl and street singer for a while (she was known as Nosegay Fan), she became servant to a French milliner. No doubt this employment helped to form that good taste in dress for which she was later famous. In August 1755, she was engaged as an actress by Theophilus Cibber at the theatre in the Haymarket and, after other theatrical engagements at Bath and Richmond, she became a member of the Drury Lane company in the 1756-57 season. She married James Abington, her music master and a royal trumpeter, but soon pensioned him off. She went to Dublin in December 1759 and remained there until 1765, when she returned to Drury Lane at Garrick's invitation.

Facially Mrs. Abington was not outstandingly attractive, though she was capable of great animation. Easy and natural in her movements, she had a very elegant form, which she would show off, as a German visitor, G.C. Lichtenberg, remarked, "with an agreeable suggestion of doing so intentionally."[1] She had acquired great skill in modulating a voice that was not naturally pleasing and she pronounced her words with a clarity that made them audible everywhere in the theatre.

Mrs. Abington's forte was comedy rather than tragedy. She could portray various types of comic character, but excelled at playing society ladies like the Widow Bellmour in Arthur Murphy's comedy *The Way to Keep Him*, or Lady Teazle in Sheridan's *The School for Scandal*, a character the dramatist created with Mrs. Abington in mind.

Garrick and Mrs. Abington did not get on at all well and there passed between them a sustained and bitter correspondence. In Garrick's view she did not have the interests of the theatre sufficiently at heart. That "worst of bad women" was his summing-up of her on an occasion when she was threatening to retire.[2]

See 39, 45, 49.

1. Lichtenberg, p. 33.

2. See *Letters,* No. 990n.

Ann Barry (1734-1801).

Mrs. Barry was the daughter of a well-to-do apothecary of Bath. Her going on the stage, following her marriage to an actor named Dancer, appalled her family. After Dancer's death she married the actor Spranger Barry, who had been her manager at the Crow Street Theatre, Dublin. They had several seasons together at Drury Lane and went to Covent Garden in 1774. Two years after her second husband's death, Mrs. Barry married a young Irish barrister named Crawford, who was so adept at spending her money that, on one occasion, her theatrical wardrobe was seized for debt.

Mrs. Barry was a great beauty with a graceful figure and rich auburn hair. She was the most versatile actress of her day. G.C. Lichtenberg's account of her brings this out:

> She can be trimly laced up like a saucy little waiting maid, and trip about so coyly and with such charming self-complacency that all the young misses and all the tall servants in the whole house lose their hearts to her; or, on the other hand, she can sweep in with a cascade of rustling and rippling silk behind her, with an upright carriage and head turned, as though her vanity impelled her to feast her eyes on the set of her train.[1]

Amongst the roles in which she excelled were, in tragedy, Cordelia in *King Lear*, Desdemona in *Othello,* and Lady Randolph in John Home's *Douglas;* in comedy, Beatrice in *Much Ado About Nothing*, Millamant in Congreve's *The Way of the World,* Lady Townley in Colley Cibber's *The Provoked Husband*, and Widow Brady in the farce *The Irish Widow*, which Garrick wrote for her.

See 46, 56.

Susannah Maria Cibber (1714-66).

Mrs Cibber was the daughter of a London upholster and the sister of Dr. Thomas Arne, the composer. She married, in 1734, the actor Theophilus Cibber, son of Colley Cibber, Poet Laureate and a distinguished man of the theatre. The marriage was a disastrous failure and Theophilus's exploitation of his wife one of the scandals of the age. He soon abandoned her to John Sloper, a young landowner, whom he was then able to sue for damages. Mrs. Cibber settled down permanently with Sloper.

Mrs. Cibber was already known as a singer before she became an actress. It was her father-in-law who saw that she had great possibilities as an actress, and, with his encouragement and instruction, she appeared in the title role of Aaron Hill's *Zara* when it was first presented at Drury Lane on 12th January 1736. So effectively did she perform the part that her husband managed to

1. Lichtenberg, p. 31.

get her salary doubled. Small, dark and slenderly built, Mrs. Cibber was still able to play youthful parts even when past fifty. Davies praises the apparent simplicity of her acting, the symmetry of her figure, the harmony of her voice and the expressiveness of her features. "In grief and tenderness," he says, "her eyes looked as if they swam in tears; in rage and despair they seemed to dart flashes of fire."[1] Contemporary writers eulogized especially her performances as Constance in *King John*, as Ophelia in *Hamlet* and as Cordelia in *King Lear*. In comedy she did not shine.

Garrick and Mrs. Cibber first played together in 1745 in James Thomson's tragedy *Tancred and Sigismunda*. They looked so like each other it was said that they could have been mistaken for brother and sister. Davies says they "were formed by nature for the illustration of each other's talents."[2] When Mrs. Cibber died, Garrick is reported to have said: "Barry and I still remain, but tragedy is dead on one side."[3]

See 8, 14, 28, 33.

Samuel Foote (1720-77).

On Foote, who was not a regular member of the Drury Lane company, see the commentary on 7.

David Garrick (1717-79).

See 2, 6, 10, 13, 26, 37, 51, 54.

Charles Holland (1733-69).

Holland was the son of the village baker at Chiswick. His first stage appearance was at Drury Lane in February, 1755, and he remained a member of the Drury Lane company until his death from smallpox. He had a manly appearance, a strong, clear voice, and he worked very hard. He modelled his acting on Garrick's and his lack of originality was his principal defect. Churchill criticises him on this score in *The Rosciad* —

> Attitude, action, air, pause, start, sigh, groan,
> He borrowed, and made use of as his own[4] —

1. Davies, II, 111-12.

2. Davies, I, 85.

3. Murphy, II, 35.

4. Lines 327-28.

and concludes, "I hate e'en Garrick thus at second hand."[1] Holland took over several of Garrick's tragic parts when Garrick was absent or unfit.

See 38.

Thomas King (1730-1805).

The son of a London tradesman, Tom King was intended for the legal profession, but ran away from a solicitor's office to turn actor, first at Tunbridge and then in booths at Windsor and elsewhere. His first appearance at Drury Lane was in 1748, as a herald in *King Lear*.

It was in comedy that King made his name, and the roles he played in a stage career which lasted till 1802 embraced the whole range of it. One of his most famous characters was Lord Ogleby in *The Clandestine Marriage*, a part which Colman had intended for Garrick but which King made triumphantly his own. As a speaker of comic prologues and epilogues, King enjoyed great popularity.

Although he spent the greater part of nine years (1750-59) in Dublin, King was a member of the Drury Lane company during most of his career. He married in 1766 Miss Baker, a dancer, who was also a member of the Drury Lane company. He assisted in the management of Drury Lane when Garrick was away from London and also when R.B. Sheridan was patentee. When Garrick retired he presented King with his stage-sword.

King could have enjoyed a handsome living but he gambled his earnings away.

See 44, 53, 55.

Jane Pope (1742-1818).

Miss Pope's father made wigs for the Drury Lane actors. When Garrick's *Lilliput*, a dramatic entertainment based on the first book of Swift's *Gulliver's Travels*, had its first performance at Drury Lane in December 1756, with a cast of children, Miss Pope was one of them. She began her stage career proper in the same theatre in 1759 and built up a considerable reputation in comedy. She was the original Polly Honeycombe (see 27) and played Beatrice to Garrick's Benedick in the royal command performance of *Much Ado About Nothing* (1765) which marked Garrick's return to the stage after his continental travels (see 37). She was also the original Mrs. Candour in Sheridan's *The School for Scandal* (1777).

1. Line 336.

Miss Pope remained at Drury Lane until her retirement in 1808. The only break in her membership of the company was the 1775-76 season. This followed a refusal by Garrick to increase her salary.

See 27.

Hannah Pritchard (1711-68).

Mrs. Pritchard's first recorded appearance as an actress was in 1733, in which year she appeared both at Bartholomew Fair and in the theatre in the Haymarket. The following year she was engaged at Drury Lane. She went on to make a name for herself in both tragedy and comedy. Among her most successful roles were Gertrude in *Hamlet,* Lady Macbeth, Beatrice in *Much Ado About Nothing,* and Millamant in Congreve's *The Way of the World,* a role which she still played to great acclaim even when age and stoutness had made her physically unsuited to it. She had a natural dignity. Contemporary accounts praise also the ease of her movements and the distinctness and pleasant modulation of her speech.

Mrs. Pritchard led an exemplary private life. Her husband was made treasurer at Drury Lane and her daughter acted there for a number of years. Mrs. Pritchard retired from the stage on 25th April 1768 and died after having enjoyed her retirement at Bath for only a few months.

See 4, 34, 42.

Margaret Woffington (1714?-60).

The daughter of an Irish bricklayer, Margaret Woffington was, in childhood, an assistant to Madame Violante, a rope-dancer. She later went on the Dublin stage, first as a dancer, then as an actress. She came to London and was engaged at Covent Garden in 1740.

A woman of great elegance and vivacity, she excelled in playing society women in comedy — Millamant in Congreve's *The Way of the World,* Lady Betty Modish in Colley Cibber's *The Careless Husband,* Maria in the same author's *The Nonjuror.* In tragedy her harsh voice was a disadvantage to her. In a male role — Sir Harry Wildair in Farquhar's *The Constant Couple* — she was outstandingly successful. It was said that one young lady made her an offer of marriage after seeing her in the part.

She was as charming off the stage as on it. She was clever in conversation, good-natured and generous. She paid for the education of her younger sister and married her off to Captain Cholmondeley. Lord Cholmondeley, the bridegroom's father, went to Woffington to complain of the marriage but she charmed him into acquiescence. She told him it was she who had the more cause to be offended: "I had one beggar to support, and now I shall have two!"[1]

Woffington was devoted to her profession. Unlike some of her colleagues, she never feigned illness out of pique or so as to get a night off. She was also quite willing to take an inferior role in a play, if this was what was required of her.

She was much fonder of the company of men than of women and explained this on the grounds that women talked of nothing except silks and scandal. She did not get on well with other leading actresses — for example, Mrs. Clive, Mrs. Cibber and Mrs. Bellamy. In 1756, when she was playing Roxana to Mrs. Bellamy's Statira in Nathaniel Lee's tragedy *The Rival Queens,* she attacked Mrs. Bellamy in such earnest when the moment was reached when she had to stab her, as to drive her nearly off the stage. The cause of her particular incensement on this occasion, it is said, was a fine dress Mrs. Bellamy had received from Paris and was wearing in the play.

Garrick and Woffington were on intimate terms when they went to Dublin in 1742 to play at the Smock Alley Theatre and they lived together for a time after they returned to London. Garrick wanted to marry her and, according to Woffington, went so far as to buy a wedding-ring and try it on her finger. But she had other lovers as well and Garrick could not get her to make the final break with them.

Woffington left Drury Lane at the end of the 1747-48 season and never returned. Playing Rosalind in *As You Like It* at Covent Garden in May 1757, she was taken ill and was not able to act again.

See 3, 5.

Henry Woodward (1717-77).

The son of a Southwark tallow-chandler, Woodward was educated at the Merchant Taylors' School. He played in *The Beggar's Opera* as one of a company of child actors, in January 1729. He was subsequently apprenticed to the actor-manager John Rich and went with him to his new theatre at Covent Garden when it opened in 1732. Rich — under the stage-name of "Lun" — was famous as Harlequin in pantomime and taught the part to Woodward, who became known as "Lun Junior". In later life Woodward was to compete with Rich in pantomimes which he devised for Garrick at Drury Lane.

1. Doran, II, 204.

Woodward's association with Drury Lane began as soon as his apprenticeship was ended and during Garrick's management he became one of the mainstays of the company. In 1758, however, his demand that his salary should never be less than that of the highest-paid actor in the company was refused and he left Drury Lane to join with Spranger Barry in the management of Crow Street Theatre, Dublin. The project failed and lost Woodward his savings. On his return to London in 1763, he engaged at Covent Garden, where he continued, with only minor breaks, until forced by illness to retire in 1776.

Off the stage Woodward was a very silent man, not in the least inclined to gaiety, but on the stage he played comic parts with extraordinary vivacity. Amongst the roles he excelled in were, as well as Harlequin, Mercutio in *Romeo and Juliet* (for which he dressed as a fine gentleman of the eighteenth century, in peruke, three-cornered hat, velvet costume, and high-heeled, gold-buckled shoes), Touchstone in *As You Like It*, Bobadil in Ben Jonson's *Every Man in His Humour,* Captain Absolute in Sheridan's *The Rivals*, and Marplot in Mrs. Centlivre's *The Busybody*. In tragedy, he was a hopeless failure – he seemed incapable of uttering a line seriously.

See 11, 47.

Mary Ann Yates (1728-87).

Mrs. Yates had appeared on the stage before her marriage to the comic actor Richard Yates, but not with any great success. With her husband, an experienced actor and her senior by twenty-two years, to coach her, she gave greatly improved performances and established herself as a member of the Drury Lane company. Her first important success was in 1759, in the role of Mandane in Arthur Murphy's tragedy *The Orphan of China*. She was given the part because of the illness of Mrs. Cibber, and Murphy is said to have rehearsed her in it himself (see commentary on 21).

As a tragic actress, Mrs. Yates had the advantage of a magnificent figure and a stately deportment and she had acquired a fine command of gesture. Her voice, though inclined to monotony, was capable of great power. In the rendering of rage and scorn she was particularly impressive. Mrs. Yates is said to have been ineffective in comedy, though her performance as Violante in Mrs. Centlivre's *The Wonder: A Woman Keeps a Secret* is well spoken of, and she appeared in this role with Garrick on the evening of his last performance.

Throughout the years, Mrs. Yates' tantrums added a good deal to Garrick's managerial burden.

See 21, 29, 31.

Elizabeth Younge (1744?-97).

Miss Younge was born in Southwark and was a milliner's apprentice before going on the stage. After her first stage appearance on 22nd October 1768, at Drury Lane, she quickly established herself. Mrs. Pritchard had retired on the 25th April of that year, so that parts which she had played were available for the new actress.

Like Mrs. Pritchard, Miss Younge was effective in both comedy and tragedy. Her comic characters were based on careful observation of life and she had great vivacity. She excelled particularly in the portrayal of aristocratic and fashionable ladies. Portia in *The Merchant of Venice* was also one of the roles in which she was greatly praised. She had very expressive features and in tragedy could communicate distress very feelingly. She played Cordelia to Garrick's Lear on the night before his retirement. After they had left the stage hand in hand, Garrick is said to have remarked that this was the last time he would ever be her father. Whereupon Miss Younge knelt down and asked for his fatherly blessing, as she had asked for it in the part of Cordelia in the play.

Her relations with Garrick were not always so cordial. An epigram published at the time of Garrick's retirement, offered, as an explanation of it, his exasperation with Miss Younge and two of her fellow-actresses:

> I have no nerves, says Y[oun]g[e]; I cannot act!
> I've lost my limbs, cries A[bingto]n; 'tis fact!
> Y[ate]s screams, I've lost my voice, my throat's so sore!
> Garrick declares he'll play the fool no more.
> Without nerves, limbs, and voice, no show, that's certain:
> Here, prompter, ring the bell, and drop the curtain.[1]

Although, certainly, not the most co-operative member of Garrick's company, Miss Younge, apart from a season in Dublin, remained at Drury Lane until 1779, three years after Garrick's retirement, going then to Covent Garden. She continued acting until January 26th 1797, less than two months before her death. She married, in 1785, the actor Alexander Pope, who was about twenty years younger than herself.

See 52.

1. Quoted Davies, II, 329.

INDEX OF FIRST LINES

Numbers refer to items of verse in this selection.

163